ABOUT THE AUTHOR

Pat Buckley, the oldest of eleven children, was born in Tullamore, County Offaly, in 1952. His father Jim started life as a labourer and through years of determination and part-time study was called to the Bar in Dublin at the age of 57. His mother Jo (76) devoted her life entirely to her family and still resides with Pat.

Wanting to be a priest since he was a child, Pat was ordained in 1976 and served as a priest in Wales and Northern Ireland. In 1986 he was removed from ministry by Cardinal Cahal Daly because of his liberal views and his expression of those views in the media.

From his Oratory in Larne, Northern Ireland, Bishop Pat ministers to people from all over Ireland, the UK and the world. He has a special ministry to divorced Catholics seeking remarriage, to the gay and lesbian community and to many people alienated by legalistic Christianities. His Episcopal motto is *Tolerance, Love, Diversity*. His mission statement is from Pope John XXIII: *"At my window a little light will always keep burning. All may come in. The arms of a friend are waiting."*

E-mail: bishoppatbuckley@hotmail.com
Website: www.bishoppatbuckley.co.uk

A SEXUAL LIFE,
A SPIRITUAL LIFE
A Painful Journey to Inner Peace

Bishop Pat Buckley

Foreword by Senator David Norris

The Liffey Press
Dublin

Published by
The Liffey Press
Ashbrook House
10 Main Street, Raheny,
Dublin 5, Ireland
www.theliffeypress.com

© 2005 Bishop Pat Buckley

A catalogue record of this book is
available from the British Library.

ISBN 1-904148-68-9

All rights reserved. No part of this publication may be reproduced or transmitted in any form or by any means, including photocopying and recording, without written permission of the publisher. Such written permission must also be obtained before any part of this publication is stored in a retrieval system of any nature. Requests for permission should be directed to The Liffey Press, Ashbrook House, 10 Main Street, Dublin 5, Ireland.

Printed in the Republic of Ireland by ColourBooks Ltd.

Contents

About the Author i
Acknowledgements vii
Foreword by Senator David Norris xi
Preface 1

Part One: A Sexual Life, A Spiritual Life

Chapter One	Origins and Destinations	19
Chapter Two	The Wounding	33
Chapter Three	An Agonising Puberty: Loneliness, Sexuality, Spirituality	51
Chapter Four	Sex in the Seminary	65
Chapter Five	Desire and Denial	83
Chapter Six	Falling In Love	95
Chapter Seven	"Coming Out"	113

Part Two: Towards a New Spirituality of Sex

Chapter Eight	The Catholic Church: Sex, Lies and Guilt	123
Chapter Nine	Jesus, Sexuality and Love	141
Chapter Ten	A New Spirituality of Sex	151

Part Three: Still a Thorn

Chapter Eleven   A Decade in My Life 175

Chapter Twelve   The Future 193

Epilogue 201

Recommended Further Reading 203

Acknowledgements

George Canning, who served in the British government of William Pitt once asked: "When our perils are past, shall our gratitude sleep?" There are few things more important in life and in human relationships than gratitude — the saying of *Thanks*.

I have so many people to be grateful to when it comes to my life in general and this book in particular. I am not a sanctimonious man but in the context of this being a book about my sexuality and spirituality I want to say first and simply that I am most grateful to God for his infinite generosity to me and his more infinite patience with me.

Secondly I must thank my mother and best friend, Jo, for over half a century of unconditional love. I also greatly appreciate the practical supportive sibling love of my sister Margaret Geoghegan, my brother John and my sister Linda McIntyre.

I want to thank other important people who were lighthouse figures to me on my life voyage. There is Fr John Hyde SJ (RIP); Canon John Pierce PP (RIP); Gerard Tuohy, my most memorable secondary school teacher; Archbishop John Charles McQuaid (RIP) my onetime confessor; Brother Gerard Collins (RIP) (Dublin and Kerry); Monsignor John Shine (Waterford); The Ursuline Sisters (Waterford); Bishop William Philbin (RIP) and Monsignor Patrick Mullally (RIP), both of the Diocese of Down and Connor, who helped me greatly in 1978 at a very difficult time in my life. I was also helped and inspired by the immense integrity of people like Fr Des Wilson (Belfast) and Fr Michael Keane (Knock Marriage Bureau).

Dr Paul McQuaid formerly of the Child Guidance Clinic at the Mater Hospital Dublin was a most compassionate "safety net" for me when I was petrified on adolescence's tightrope in the early 1960s. Dr Paul and I have recently renewed our contact after nearly forty years.

I am most grateful to all my former parishioners at St Peter's, Belfast; Kilkeel, County Down; and Larne, County Antrim, who have kept me in their esteem and prayers for nearly twenty years now.

I am especially grateful to all my loyal friends and associates at The Oratory in Larne who have stuck by me through thick and thin since 1985. Their love and support have kept me afloat through many a storm. I am very thankful to my hermit priest colleague Mother Frances Meigh of Armagh, who from her mountain fastness prays and supports my ministry.

In the preparation of this book for publication I want to thank those who expressed interest, offered support and read drafts. My newly ordained colleague Fr Ed Kenneally was a Martha to my Mary and performed a myriad of small but very important tasks for me.

I am grateful to The Liffey Press for having the courage and imagination to publish a book by a controversial author on a potentially very controversial topic. I thank David Givens, Liffey Press proprietor and Heidi Murphy in marketing. I owe a special debt of gratitude to editor Brian Langan. Pat Buckley is not an easy author to edit but Brian handled the lion in his den with an utter professionalism and a lot of the "polish" on this book, if it is a diamond at all, is down to Brian the polisher.

Finally I want to express my undying thanks to Senator David Norris for his Foreword. We imposed a ridiculously short deadline on David and at a time when he was suffering from a nasty chest infection. But in spite of these constraints the Foreword is what I would describe as vintage Norris. David Norris is himself a towering figure in Irish society when it comes to qualities like tolerance, the pursuit of justice and the enthronement of compassion, truth and integrity in public life. I am both humbled and honoured that Senator David Nor-

Acknowledgements

ris of Trinity College, Dublin, an international Joycean scholar, would write a Foreword to a book written by someone like me.

Now I rest my pen and await with tranquil interest and anticipation the most important judgement of all — the judgement of the reader. If this book helps even one person, then with my beloved Hafiz I will pour a glass of wine and exclaim: "We keep each other happy and warm."

Foreword

Senator David Norris

Pat Buckley, Priest, Iconoclast, Bishop, is an extraordinary man with a prophetic voice and a strong ego. A prophetic voice is necessary if the church is to be of any relevance to young people in the twenty-first century and the ego is equally necessary to protecting a man like Bishop Buckley against mean side-swipes from the Church establishment, for he was always a thorn in the side of the hierarchy.

I have met Pat Buckley on a number of occasions over the last ten years. The thing that has always struck me most forcibly about him is his searing honesty and absolute sincerity even when his championing of the truth could lead him into personal difficulties. And this book is a valuable expression of these qualities. The pity is that it was written by someone who has been forced to be an outsider even while remaining tenuously inside the church. What a wonderful day of revelation and hope it would have been if this book could have been written by any Bishop, Cardinal or theologian in good standing with the Vatican. But this would be too much to expect. The Christian Churches have all without exception lied and equivocated about the truth of human sexuality for their own squalid purposes and none have lied more consistently than the Roman Catholic Church. It grieves me to say this but the evidence is all around us. The establishment of a Commission by Pope Paul VI to report to him on the matter of contraception, and his subsequent rejection of the unanimous view expressed by this Commission of Experts, lay, clerical and medical, is a classic example. The campaign against condoms in Africa which undoubtedly leads to the spread of Aids is yet another, and of course the unrelenting and unchristian attacks on gay people with the virulent language employed — "objectively evil", "intrinsically disordered", "virus", etc. — are a shame and a reproach to anyone who understands the Gospel message of love.

Of course, telling the truth is not the best method of securing advancement in the Church. A list of the late twentieth-century victims of the Holy Office — Archbishop Hunthausen, Archbishop Romero, Professor Dr John McNeill, Dr Charles Curran, Professor Hans Küng, Leonard Boff — reads like a roll of honour of the great spiritual thinkers of the Church.

Bishop Buckley (and to the annoyance of Church authorities their own view of the apostolic succession must lead them to acknowledge that he is indeed a Bishop) has decided to write this book to express views that are, as he says, "forged not only at the forge of intellectual and emotional introspection and reflection but also at the forge of daily lived experience". Once again there are dangers here, as one can see from the title *A Sexual Life, A Spiritual Life: A Painful Journey to Inner Peace*. Bishop Buckley recounts how he was warned by a friend to whom he revealed that he was writing an honest book about his own sexuality and the spiritual lessons he had learnt from it: "Your enemies will gather like wasps around a jam jar, and you will only be giving them ammunition." Perhaps indeed that is true but I have sufficient confidence in the decency and humanity of the Irish people, to believe that his openness will place the majority of people on the side of the Bishop and against the wasps.

The dedication of the book to all those whose sexuality brought them pain, guilt and confusion and his wish for those who sow in sorrow to sing when they reap indicates the importance of his audience. That audience is the ordinary people, those who have been burdened with guilt by a Church that is, as he says, "too male, too patriarchal and too clerical". The Bishop himself comes from a representative

Irish background. He was born in the midlands at the beginning of the 1950s into a family where his mother, like many observant Catholic women of that period, seemed endlessly to produce babies — seventeen in her case. These women were the heroines and sometimes the martyrs of Irish family life. This background and the classic Catholic guilt about sexual appetite that was instilled in the young Pat Buckley enables him to say with conviction that "The Catholic Church as always used sex to control and dominate people. We, the people, have let them away with it." The book is in a sense a rallying cry to end this oppression.

We get an insight into the prevailing ethos in a couple of little vignettes. There is the figure of the late Archbishop Dr John Charles McQuaid and his fireside chats with young seminarians from Clonliffe. They would be summoned for face-to-face meetings with the Archbishop in his study. The queasily prurient nature of these talks has been recorded elsewhere but the powerful picture presented here by Bishop Buckley suggests that Dr McQuaid was a lonely rather pathetic figure who was actually unaware of his own sexual motivation and certainly would not have agreed with St Bonaventure, who is quoted as saying, "The mind's road to God always begins in the sexual appetite."

When Bishop Buckley writes about sex he approaches the mystic and for some people this may be shocking, but many of the medieval Mystics also used sexual imagery to describe the ecstasy of religious experience. Bishop Buckley suggests, for example, that the moment of orgasm is in fact a glimpse of the deity. Some people may find this surprising but again if people are honest I think they will recognise the very human truth in this.

Surveys quoted in this book suggest that in the United States a considerable majority of vowed religious acknowledge that they are sexually active. Ten per cent of priests state that they were propositioned in their seminaries and at least thirty per cent of Catholic priests in the United States have homosexual orientation. What a pity the

Church cannot face up to this reality in an honest way, but then it is as we are told in this book, "a two-thousand-year-old human empire".

Some people may be shocked by subjects honestly encountered in this book, especially matters such as the sexuality of Jesus Christ himself. Bishop Buckley acknowledges that even asking questions about the sexuality of the son of God can be seen as blasphemous. But it seems to me that if one reads these passages with an open mind, what one will be struck by is the very sane and commonsensical way in which the matter is approached. Furthermore, the good Bishop is content to acknowledge that there are some areas in which he simply cannot give a clear answer. Some people will be disturbed by statements about Christ such as: "If he was one hundred per cent human that means his body was exactly like the body of every other man who lived before him or who has lived since. That means that Jesus had genitalia — a penis and two testicles." However, if we stand back and look at this, it is a perfectly ordinary statement and Christ would have made a very strange fish indeed if he were arranged any differently.

I hope that young people will buy and read this book for its honesty, decency and humanity. For many people troubled with guilt about their sexuality, I believe it will be a balm.

Senator David Norris
4 May 2005

This book is dedicated to those of every time and place for whom sexuality was or is, for whatever reason, a source of agony and pain. May those who sow in tears sing when they reap.

*"Whoever survives a test,
whatever it may be,
must tell the story"*

— Elie Wiesel

Preface

A Sexual Life, A Spiritual Life

MOST THINKING MEN DESIRE to give at least one account of themselves and their life, an account that will live on after they have gone. In my sermons I have told my congregations: "As a snail crosses your path, he leaves his trail. If a humble snail leaves a trail should not those of us who are human — sons and daughters of God — leave our trail too?" Surely the saddest thing that could be said of any human being would be: "He left no mark on the world. His effect on the world and on life amounted to nothing?" Were that to be my epitaph I think I would ask God to let me spend eternity in an empty corner of Heaven, weeping. The poet Stephen Williams wrote:

> They die not, for they lived not; under earth
> Their bodies urge the meaner flowers to birth:
> Unstung, unfired, untempted was their soul,
> Easy extinction is their utmost goal.

Is it pride, vanity and ego that makes a person want to write a book as an apologia? They do, at least in part, for me. But I think it is much more the conviction that one was given a destiny to fulfil and the apologia is something of a self-examination of how well or how poorly one fulfilled that destiny, that call. In this context, I fully embrace Cardinal Newman's great prayer:

> God has created me to do some definite service; He has committed some work to me which He has not committed to another. I have my mission; I may never know it in this life, but I shall be told it in the next. I have a part in a great work; I am a link in a chain, a bond of

connection between persons. He has not created me for naught. I shall do good, I shall do His work; I shall be an angel of peace, a preacher of truth in my own place, while not intending it, if I do but keep His commandments.

At this stage on my journey, it is my belief that God sent me into the world and into the Catholic Church to be a "prophet" and a "dissident". At my baptism while anointing my head with the blessed Oil of Chrism, the priest said to me: "As Christ was anointed priest, prophet and king, so may you live always as a member of his body, sharing everlasting life." Every Christian is supposed to share in Christ's priesthood, prophecy and kingship. But most of us don't know this or we forget it.

Now a prophet is not someone who foretells the future. A prophet is someone who has a message and declares and attempts to live out that message — whether the message is welcome or unwelcome. True prophets are usually unwelcome. They call for change and the herd of humanity resists change. As Christ said: "Woe to you when the world speaks well of you; this was the way their fathers treated the false prophets. Blessed are you when the world reviles you; this was the way their fathers treated the true prophets."

Nor indeed is the prophet perfect, sinless or always psychologically stable. The Old Testament is full of prophets who were most imperfect, as sinful as any other and certainly eccentric. But none of that stops them being God's messengers. For Christ Himself said that He would use the weak to confound the strong; that He would use what the world thinks foolish to confound the wise; and that He would use those of "ill repute" to confound the so-called "respectable".

As a "prophet", I am most imperfect, undeniably a sinner and open to the charge of eccentricity. But I am reminded of that occasion when at a clergy conference a priest complained to the local bishop about St John Vianney, the Curé of Ars and the patron saint of priests: "My Lord, Father Vianney is mad." The good bishop thought a while and replied, "I wish the rest of you were half as mad."

Preface

As I write of myself as a prophet, I can hear the questions rising in some readers' minds: "Is this man for real? Does he have delusions of grandeur?" These are valid questions. But please read the whole book before you make up your mind. If I know and believe things to be true and don't say them because I am afraid of being misunderstood, misjudged or written off as "unbalanced", then I would only be writing a politically correct book to impress. I am not interested at all in doing that. I am telling things as they were and are. I am telling the truth, the whole truth and nothing but the truth. Maybe spiritual things are often thought to be crazy in this world? In the New Testament we are told that the family of Jesus came to take him home, thinking he was mad!

I am not one of those who does not question himself. I constantly question, and analyse my beliefs and my motives and actions. And the kind of reading I do constantly challenges me too. One of my heroes, Fr George Tyrrell SJ, challenges me a lot with such passages as the following one from his biography by Maud Petre:

> Enclosed saddens me [he writes in May 1902, referring to some utterance of a religious leader], especially in the light of his mental breakdown at the end. He seems to have yielded himself to the belief in his own mission without any sort of criticism of self-distrust; without any fear of fanaticism or illusion. Of course this self-belief is the secret of such success as he effected. But, dear me! How strange it seems! Perhaps if he had more moral difficulties and defects it might have awakened a wholesome self-criticism. To think oneself an instrument of God's designs — a privilege one shares with the devil — is a reasonable reflection, if not very profitable; but to view oneself as a special instrument, as a sort of miraculous providence, seems to me the most dangerous sort of fanaticism, not to say pride. And yet the saints have been full of it!

These thoughts of George Tyrrell are most challenging for me as someone who is going against the mainstream church and who believes that this is what God wants me to do. And this is how I would respond to Fr Tyrrell's challenge.

I do believe in my mission. But each day I have many thoughts of self-criticism. I am not fanatical. I am totally anti-fanaticism in all aspects of life — religious, political and social. And I don't suffer from illusions. I understand that pride was the sin of Satan and it is a great trap for us all. I regard myself as an instrument of God's designs but not as a *special* instrument in the sense that I am better than any other servant. I am painfully aware too that I am a most sinful instrument. In fact I am just a Balaam's Ass (Book of Numbers 22: 22–35).

Bishop (now Cardinal) Cahal Daly did accuse me during my protracted dispute with him of being "mentally unbalanced" and of having "a saviour complex". I will speak more of Cahal Daly later but in the meantime would refer him to the John Vianney story above.

What of Mary Magdala's claim to have seen the Risen Christ on Easter Sunday morning? Did the cynics in Jerusalem or the male apostles think she was just a hysterical woman having delusions? What did the cynics make of the persecutor of Christians, Paul, and his mystical meeting with Christ and his conversion on the road to Damascus? Was Paul developing a saviour complex? What did the cynics in Assisi and Rome think of St Francis's mystical experiences? Did they accuse him of delusions of grandeur and of hysteria? What did the cynical and corrupt Carmelite monks think of the mysticism of St Teresa of Avila and St John of the Cross and their efforts to reform the religious order. Did they accuse them of delusion? Was John's Ascent of Mount Carmel the product of an unbalanced mind? Did the recently canonised Padre Pio create his stigmata out of some pathological psychology?

These are all valid questions for anyone to ask who wants to go down the path of accusing anyone else of hysteria, delusions or of having a saviour complex.

And who would claim that God has stopped choosing, communicating with and using people just because it is the Third Millennium? Have we arrived at that point in society and in the Church when we say: "God never chooses people anymore. He never asks people to do a certain mission. He has stopped communicating heart-to-heart with individuals. The Holy Spirit has retired!" If that is where we have arrived, then God is not dead as our friend Nietzsche said, but the soul of man most certainly is.

WHAT HAS BEEN AND IS MY MESSAGE? My message is that what Christ founded was a kingdom and what has evolved is a church. My message is that over nineteen centuries men have continuously added on the thinking of men to the point where the original Christian community is hardly visible. My message is that the radical and liberal message of Christ has been transformed by power-hungry men into authoritarian and institutionalised doctrine and that the Scriptures have been forced into second place in the Catholic Church (and all churches) by the man-made Code of Canon Law. My message is that the church is too male, too patriarchal and too clerical. And my message is that the radical Christ would want the nineteen centuries of distortion stripped away and a return to the charismatic kingdom he founded. And of course this message has profound repercussions for our sexuality, our spirituality and for morality, women, collegiality and every pastoral practice in the church.

Why am I a dissident? I believe that I had dissidence thrust upon me by God and that it was and is my destiny. As such, it is both my joy and my cross. It is profoundly my vocation.

Being a dissident is at once a severely painful special calling and a great blessing. It is the Scriptural call to go outside the gate, to stand with Christ who was put outside the gate and camp by the religious leaders, high priests and respectable people of his day. I used to feel a little sorry for myself that I was outside the camp (the priestly, hierarchical one) until I read Fr John McNeill's beautiful words about how important it is for us dissident Christians to embrace our exile status:

> We must be prepared to accept our exile state both within society and within the Church. We must grieve and gradually let go of the desire to "belong" to all the institutions of this world. We must deepen our spiritual roots and our realisation that in direct proportion to our exile

state in this world, we belong in a deeper and more cosmic level to a community bound together by God's love and God's mercy.

Jesus was crucified outside the gates of Jerusalem. In fact, He was crucified on the city dump.

Those of us who are "outside" the gate of Rome are experiencing from Rome and its legalistic and power-crazy clerics what Jesus experienced at the hands of the legalistic and power-crazy clerics of Jerusalem. Different cities, same syndrome! But we can take heart from Christ's words: "Where the Master is there also will be his servants."

Most Christians have abandoned or suppressed the so-called "apocryphal gospels" — the other gospels and writings that existed alongside our present New Testament at the beginning of the Church and for the first centuries of the Church — and indeed most Christians are not even aware of their existence. In one of those "gospels", the *Acts of Paul*, we read, "He [Paul] hired a barn outside Rome for his first service." While I am very much a part of God and Christ's Catholic Church, I am aware that I have been pushed outside the Catholic Church as a structure and institution and outside its man-made Canon Law. I like the idea of being in a barn outside Rome. First of all, it is situated in "greater Rome" but still outside Rome as narrowly defined. Secondly, Jesus was born in a barn and if we are with Him outside the gate is it not very appropriate to share His type of birthplace too?

Nowhere is the diverging of the institutional Church from the original intentions of Jesus Christ more evident than in the area of human sexuality, and specifically in the tragic separation of sex and spirit. This theme has been at the core of my life, and is at the core of this book.

Sex and Spirit

"The mind's road to God always begins in the sexual appetite." These words were written by none other than the Franciscan theologian and mystic St Bonaventure who has long since being declared a Doctor of the Church. Bonaventure also served as Master General of the Franciscan Order and was a cardinal. His mystical theology has inspired not only the Franciscans but also the Dominicans, Carthusians and the Brothers of the Common Life. Pope Leo XIII said that when it came to mystical theology, Bonaventure was *facile princes* — "the first in his field".

Bonaventure realised that sexuality and spirituality are irrevocably intertwined and cannot be separated without doing great harm to an individual both spiritually and psychologically. The English mystic, Julian of Norwich (1342–1416) concurred with Bonaventure and took it a step further when she wrote:

> God is the means whereby our Substance and our Sensuality are kept together so as never to be apart. Both our Substance and our Sensuality together may rightly be called our Soul. That is because they are both one in God. Our Sensuality is the beautiful City in which Our Lord Jesus sits and in which He is enclosed.

For Julian the sexual and the spiritual are quite simply two parts of the very soul itself — the soul that has been created by God and infused into us at the moment of our conception; the immortal soul that is destined to live eternally with God in Heaven.

The soul is only truly itself when it exists in peace and harmony. We know from the Bible and our Christian theology that the Holy Spirit is present in someone when that person has inner peace and harmony. There is peace and harmony in the soul when sensuality and spirituality are living happily together. If sensuality and spirituality are not integrated and happily co-existing, the soul is disturbed and not at peace. The retired priest, psychotherapist and author Richard Sipe quoted in his book *Celibacy*:

> Sexuality can be homeless for a Christian who has failed to integrate his sexuality into his life as a Christian. If to be redeemed by Christ is to be fully human, if to be truly holy is to be truly whole with an integrated human nature, any fragmentation of our sexuality is a sign that we need healing, that we need to be made whole and holy. And

so any genuinely Christian spirituality must help us to affirm our human sexuality.

Others from the Christian tradition, apart from Bonaventure and Julian, have attested to the unity of substance and spirit, sexuality and spirituality, body and soul, and to the goodness of the body and sex. In the Bible the author of the *Songs of Songs* (7: 9–12) speaks of:

> Wine flowing straight to my Beloved,
> as it runs on the lips of those who sleep.
> I am my Beloved's,
> And his desire is for me.
> Come, my Beloved,
> Let us go to the fields.
> We will spend the night in the villages,
> And in the morning we will go to the vineyards.

Saint Mechtild of Magdeburg (1209–1283) wrote:

> Do not disdain your body.
> For the soul is just as safe in its body
> As it is in the Kingdom of Heaven.

Meister Eckhart (1260–1328) wrote: "The soul loves the body."

A true grasp of the Bible and of the mind of Christ would never seek to separate sexuality and spirituality and thereby do such terrible violence to the human soul. The splitting up of body and soul, sexuality and spirituality, has no basis in the Old Testament on which the Judeo-Christian faith is founded. The dualistic theology of body and soul and the destructive theology of "original sin" only developed in the early centuries of Christianity and under the influence of the reformed playboy theologian St Augustine of Hippo (354–430). Professor Herbert Haag, former president of the Catholic Bible Association of Germany and author of *Is Original Sin in Scripture?* says:

> The doctrine of original sin is not found in any of the writings of the Old Testament. . . . This ought to be recognised today not only by Old Testament scholars but also by dogmatic theologians. . . . The idea that Adam's descendants are automatically sinners because of the sin of

> their ancestor, and that they are already sinners when they enter the world, is foreign to Holy Scripture. No man enters the world a sinner. As the creature and image of God he is from his first hour surrounded by God's fatherly love. Consequently, he is not at birth, as is often maintained, an enemy of God and a child of God's wrath. A man becomes a sinner only through his own individual and responsible action.

So to be humanly happy and happy as Christians we must integrate our sexuality and our spirituality. We must come to know that our body is good as well as our soul. We must know that our sexuality and sensuality are the products of the spark of God within us. We must know that when we use our sexuality in a loving and non-abusive way we are "pro-creators" — participants in the work of God the Creator. We must know that our body is holy, that our sex drive is holy, that our genitalia are holy and that our sexual energy is a spiritual thing and is a small share in the Divine Energy which is God. We must also know that the moment of ecstasy we experience when we have an orgasm is a brief and very pale glimpse of the indescribable ecstasy we will experience when we see God for the first time and live with Him eternally.

The implication of knowing and believing all this is that we must re-think all we have been taught in Christianity and Catholicism about our bodies and our sexuality being dirty and sinful. Instead of believing that sex is a sin which separates us from God, we must believe that sex is a God-given gift that brings us towards God and unites us with Him. In fact, we must come to see that our sexuality and our sex life is a prayer to God, a way of worshipping God — "with my body I Thee worship".

Of course, there *is* a sexual morality. We are morally bound to use all God's gifts to do good and not evil. Sexuality if abused or wrongly used can be a sin in the eyes of God. The gift of our sexuality is in itself good. But we can misuse and abuse it.

Like so many others, I was given a very negative view of my body and my sexuality as a child and as a teenager. As a child I was taught that nakedness was a negative thing and that one's private parts were dark, mysterious and bad things that must never be thought about, never mind looked at or touched. From the beginning, I was ashamed of my body.

Later on in school and confession and college I learned more about how "bad" the body and sex were. I was told that "impure thoughts" were a serious sin and that I must count each one and tell the priest in confession the thoughts I had. It was terrible going to confession in my teens and having to confess hundreds of impure thoughts!

I was also told that touching myself or masturbating were "mortal sins" — sins that cut me off completely from God and would bring me straight to hell if I died before getting to confession. As a teenager I was running to confession three or four times a week!

And of course sexual contact with somebody else was a sin so serious that there were hardly words to describe it. I was twenty-one before I had a voluntary sexual experience with anyone. It happened in the dark of night with another young man my age. We hardly did anything and all in all I'm sure it lasted twenty seconds, if that. But, having spent the night crying and shivering in bed, filled with remorse, guilt and self-loathing, I woke a priest up at seven in the morning to get my mortal sin wiped out.

My negative attitude to sex was greatly strengthened by my seminary studies of moral theology. When I was ordained at twenty-four I felt that the priest and the soul in me had to fight every second of every day and night against my body and the sexual demons that inhabited it. Sexually, psychologically, spiritually, I was the slave of a personal identity crisis that made me half-mad. I was deeply unhappy. My soul was constantly at war and the tug of war was between my body and my soul, my spirituality and my sensuality, my life of prayer and meditation and my raging sexual desires. All this time my prayer and spirituality was all about acknowledging my wickedness, and begging forgiveness. Spiritually I had no joy and no peace and I concluded that this was the way God wanted me to live, my private crucifixion, my share in the sufferings of Christ on the cross.

Preface

It would take me to the age of forty-seven before I came to know and understand with Bonaventure that "the mind's road to God begins in the sexual appetite". The thirty-five years between twelve and forty-seven were thirty-five years of hell. I would not want to pass through that dark valley again but looking back I can see that all the pain was not wasted. The humanity, understanding and compassion I have as a priest is one of the precious fruits of all that pain. I know that gold, to be purified, must undergo the fire and the furnace. I am aware of how my thirty-five-year furnace has "purified" my heart and brought me to a very deep place before God.

I also observe many priests I know who did not go through the furnace. Theirs was an easier passage. But I also see, with sadness, the spiritual and pastoral poverty and shallowness of many of them, and I would not swap places with them. Of course, I would have enjoyed the raw pleasure but I would not have liked to be sexually "liberated" and active in the seminary and immediately after. I think you only appreciate the "promised land" when you have languished a long time in the desert. The man who has spent a long time hungry appreciates the banquet more than the man who has never known hunger and who has dined finely every day for years.

Writing this Book

When I told a close friend that I was writing this book he said that he was very worried for me. Here was a Catholic priest and bishop writing a public confession of his struggle with his sexuality. "Your enemies will gather like wasps around a jam jar," he protectively said, "and you will only be giving them ammunition."

I can understand my friend's caution and fear. And I publish this book with a little fear and trepidation. But the Jesus that I poorly try to follow tells me that "the truth will set you free". This book is proof that I take Him at His word.

To those armchair critics or "hurlers on the ditch" who would seek to abuse my honesty I would like to address the deeply spiritual words of Monsignor Bernard Powers of Milwaukee:

Who Am I to Judge?

I have not heard
Your unique call to creation
Nor seen the image you are to reveal . . .
How can I judge you?

I have not tasted
The Bitterness of your burdens
Nor the gall of your crucifixion . . .
How can I condemn you?

I have not felt
The strength of your efforts
Nor known the intensity of your battles . . .
How can I ridicule you?

I have not known the agony
Of your thirst
Nor the heat of your passions
Nor the burning desires of your nature . . .
How can I criticise you?

I have not climbed
The mountains of your life
Nor walked the valleys of your experiences
Nor endured the torture of your desert . . .
How can I despise you?

I have not heard all that you said
Nor witnessed all that you did . . .
How can I say you are not true?

I have not suffered your silence
Not felt your loneliness
Nor your isolation . . .
How can I reject you?

I have not known
The touch of your environment
Nor the struggles of your youth
Nor the burdens of your day . . .
How can I say you should not have fallen?

I have not prayed in your garden . . .
Worn your crown . . .
Endured your scourging . . .

> Carried your cross . . .
> Suffered your Crucifixion . . .
> Who am I that I should judge you?
> My sister, my brother,
> Here are my hands
> In tender compassion.

In other words: "Let him who is without sin cast the first stone."

It has been therapeutic for me to tell the truth and to be open about my sexuality — the sexuality that for years was a source of the most painful guilt and repression for me. In my previous book *A Thorn in the Side* I said that I burned my ecclesiastical bra. With this book I want to abandon and burn the suffocating corset of sexual guilt and fear.

But this book is not a selfish enterprise. I want to help others with it. I want people to read of my struggle with my sexuality and see how I have journeyed to freedom and thereby inspire others to make a similar journey — a journey from the darkness of guilt and repression to the light of openness, honesty, self-acceptance and even self-celebration. That is why it is not simply an apologia, a "confession". While the first and final parts of the book are about my personal struggle, this book is not just about "me". In the middle section of the book — its core — I tentatively offer a new way forward for those going through a similar struggle. What I am trying to suggest is that we need to reverse the damaging split between sex and spirit, and I therefore offer a new spirituality of sex, and a new sexuality of spirit.

If small-minded people or those whom my friend termed my "enemies" want to use and abuse this book, then so be it. At least, for all my human frailty — and God knows there's plenty of that — I am open and honest. I am not a pretender or a hypocritical "company man".

I know that all reasonable and right-thinking people will read this book in a spirit of openness and compassion. As for the others: "There are none so blind as those who do not wish to see."

Why I Describe my Personal Encounters/Relationships

In discussing my personal relationships with people in some chapters, I have changed all names and have changed sufficient detail so that these people are not identified.

In no way do I wish to engage in any type of "kiss-and-tell" exercise. I simply see these encounters as very important milestones on my sexual/spiritual journey and I think not to give practical but sensitive accounts of my encounters and relationships would be to take refuge in an intellectual and cerebral approach that would leave me wide open to the charge often made against celibate Catholic priests — that, having no experience of sexual intimacy and relationships, they are talking of things about which they have no real knowledge. I want to show as clearly as I can, without being coarse, that my views on sexuality and spirituality have been forged not only at the forge of intellectual and emotional introspection and reflection but also at the forge of daily lived experience. It would be so easy when dealing with sexuality and spirituality to be "so heavenly minded as to be no earthly use".

Nor indeed am I seeking to boast of experiences or give the impression of flaunting what is basically a private side of life. I simply want this book to be as open and honest as possible and to achieve that I felt challenged to nail my colours to the mast and lay down for the reader not simply my sincerely held views but also an account of how I struggled with these evolving views in the context of interpersonal relationships and my search for human love and intimacy and in the context of faith and my relationship with God.

I view everybody I mention, albeit anonymously, with all due reverence and as very important messengers and teachers on my sexual/spiritual journey.

A Statement of Faith

For my previous book, *A Thorn in the Side* I sat down and worked out what my life creed is and I include it here again as a summary of my faith and because many people have contacted me to say they liked it and agreed with it.

A Personal Creed

I believe that in this world it is impossible to understand God.
I believe that God made this wonderful universe and all that exists.
I can find God in nature, in animals, in birds and the environment.
I believe that God made all men and women,
That he made them all equal
And that he loves and cherishes them all equally.
I believe that the whole human race is the family of God.
I believe that there may be intelligent life on other planets
And if so they too are part of God's family.
I hold that religion and faith are two different things,
That religion can be both good and bad
And that it is spirituality that counts.
For me your religion is an accident of your birth
Or a gift of God's great providential diversity.
There is no one true church.
All churches and all religions contain aspects of the truth.
But only God is truth.
No man is infallible.
A Buddhist or a good atheist is as acceptable to God as a good Catholic.
I believe that sex is good and so is the body.
The only sexual act that is sinful is the one that uses or abuses.
I believe in people, especially suffering people.
I believe in the power of weakness.
I believe that all men and women will be saved.
I believe in a packed Heaven and an empty Hell.
And even Satan might get another chance.
I believe in the freedom of God's sons and daughters.
I believe that dogma is often evil.
I believe that life is a journey towards God,
And that no one has the right to insist that you go a certain road.
I believe that God and reality are too big for my poor words,
I believe therefore that I am only at a beginning,
Only knocking at a door,
And I believe that the best is yet to come.

Part One

A Sexual Life, A Spiritual Life

Chapter One

ORIGINS AND DESTINATIONS

"The little child just emerging from the pulpy embryonic forms of babyhood and looking, through wondering eyes, on the scene of incomprehensible confusion all around it." — George Tyrrell SJ

IN THE LATE 1970S I went on a primal therapy course in Nottingham, run by Dr Frank Lake. I was there for almost two weeks. We went through our whole lives with a fine comb — from the moment of conception to the present — reliving all the key moments. It was a painful and harrowing but a freeing experience.

My mother Jo has written: "Pat was born in my father's house in Tullamore, County Offaly, Ireland at 6.00 am on Friday 2 May 1952. When I looked at him I thought he was beautiful. But I also saw something that I couldn't put words to. I suppose I thought he was a present from God."

At the course all of us "relived", through breathing exercises and our conscious and subconscious imaginations, our time in the womb and our birth experience. I experienced the freedom and security of the womb. I experienced the panic and trauma of my birth, being pushed out into the world, which I was able to connect to my later insecurities and panics. Somehow I was more at peace with the deeper and darker side of my being on my return from Nottingham. So real was my experience that I was able to come home and remind my mother of things that had happened at my birth that she had forgotten.

Most children resist birth. They have come to feel safe, for nine months, in the happiness and comfort of the womb. Then labour begins and the child senses and fears change and expulsion — an end to life as he knows it. He is afraid. He panics. He fears annihilation. It is the mirror image of what will happen to him at the other end of his life when he will be "pushed" out of this world and into the next. Birth is a sister trauma to death. And we have no control over either; nature and Providence decide that the time has come.

I went on the primal therapy course because in later life I was having severe anxiety and panic attacks and wanted to try to find out why I was having them. In the anxiety and panic I experienced before and during birth I found the archetypal source of all my later panic and anxiety. That knowledge helped me cope greatly. Sometimes just understanding something or facing up to it can help greatly.

But where does all of this fit into my spiritual journey? I have always loved and personally owned the call of Jeremiah the prophet:

> A word of Yahweh came to me. "Before I formed you in the womb I knew you; before you were born I set you apart, and appointed you a prophet to the nations!"
>
> I said, "Ah, Lord Yahweh! I do not know how to speak; I am a child!"
>
> But Yahweh replied, "Do not say: "I am a child". Go now to all those I send you; and say what I command you. Do not be afraid of them, for I am with you to protect you – it is Yahweh who speaks!"
>
> Then Yahweh stretched out his hand and touched my mouth and said to me,
>
> "Now I have put my words into your mouth. See today I give you authority over nations and over kingdoms
>
> to uproot and pull down
> to destroy and overthrow,
> to build and to plant. (Jeremiah 1: 4–10).

Throughout my whole life, whenever I have heard these words from Jeremiah, something I cannot explain stirs within me and in my very soul I know they are for me as well as for Jeremiah.

I know that before I was conceived or born I was called to be a servant of God. As soon as I could speak, at the age of three, I told my mother: "Mammy, I'm going be a priest." For half a century since I was born I have never wanted to do anything else or be anything else. So I know spiritually that God created me with a vocation and a call at my very core.

Like Jeremiah I have often protested. I am the weakest of men. I am a sinner and have always lived with a very complicated inferiority complex. And yet I have fought and struggled as if I was not like that at all. My ministry has been very much about "uprooting", "pulling down", "destroying" and "overthrowing". But it has also been about "building" and "planting".

I MAY HAVE RELIVED MY BIRTH with Dr Lake in Primal Therapy but of course I have no memory whatsoever of my baptism which occurred within days of my birth at the Church of the Assumption, Tullamore, County Offaly. The church of my baptism, and indeed of my parents' marriage, was burned down some years ago and has been replaced by a very expensive modern building. It's a fine building but it does not have the atmosphere the old church had. But the church registers did not perish in the fire and a few years ago I asked the parish priest to let me have a look at my baptism entry. It was a strange feeling, in the good sense, looking at the record of my spiritual re-birth and my membership of the Catholic Church.

My parents and all my family circle attended Sunday Mass, and some of them went every day. I know I would have been to Mass regularly and that at other times I would have been brought into church to light candles, but I have few specific childhood memories of going to church. To this day I call into little lonely country churches to light a candle as I drive around the country. Even though I've never smoked, I carry a cigarette lighter in the car to light the candles as often there are no others lit. I'm always very disappointed when I find that a church does not have candles. Lighting candles is a profound symbol of my spirituality and began when I was a child.

Somehow I feel that a lit candle can say something to God that words cannot say. In the consummation of the candle before God I see my life being consumed with and for Him too. After I leave a church I continue to think of the candle burning away and my praise of God continuing with it.

Between my granny Kate, my Mam and Dad and my teacher Mother Mary Carmel of the Mercy Sisters, Carlow, I learned a few "formal" prayers that I said every day and still say today. One was the Morning Offering:

> O Jesus, through the most pure heart of Mary, I offer you all my thoughts words, sufferings and actions of this day for the intentions of your Sacred Heart.

A second prayer I learned and say was the "Prayer to My Guardian Angel":

> O Angel of God, my guardian dear, to whom God's love commits me here, ever this day (night) be at my side, to light and guard, to rule and guide. Amen.

A final prayer I learned was a prayer to the Holy Family:

> Jesus, Mary and Joseph, I give you my heart and my soul;
> Jesus, Mary and Joseph, assist me now and in my last agony;
> Jesus, Mary and Joseph, may I pour forth my soul in peace with you.
> Into thy hands O Lord I commend my spirit.
> Lord Jesus, receive my soul. Amen.

I also of course learned the Act of Contrition, Acts of Faith, Hope and Love, and the Memorare Prayer to Our Lady. Very early in life I learned to "do" the Stations of the Cross and to this day I love that devotion. And of course I learned the Rosary.

MY PATERNAL GRANDMOTHER was Kate (Catherine) Buckley (née Bracken) from Pullough just outside Tullamore in County Offaly. I was her first grandchild and from the beginning we were extremely close. I learned to say my prayers on her knee and in those days, before Ireland had television (my granny didn't even have a radio, or a bathroom or a toilet) she spent many evenings reading to me from a magazine dedicated to the Dominican, Blessed (now Saint) Martin de Porres. She read me the accounts of Blessed Martin's life and miracles, and his love of animals. And she read me the letters of thanks from people who had received favours through the intercession of Blessed Martin. I fell in love with Blessed Martin and wanted to be like him — except I wanted to be a priest and he was "only" a brother! In later life I contemplated entering the Dominican Order and attended vocation retreats with them in Tallaght, Dublin, but that was not to be.

In my granny's house, the nightly Rosary was obligatory. She ordered us all down on our knees on the stone floor with our beads. It was her one steely convention. And she would plot to rope visitors and strangers in — and especially people who were known to be not religious. As well as the formal Rosary, my granny had further prayers to add at the end. These were known all over Ireland as "trimmin's". The scene in my granny's house is perfectly described in the poem "The Trimmin's on the Rosary". It is too long to quote here in full but is available in a book called *Around the Boree Log* by "John O'Brien", published in 1957 — five years after my birth. But I quote a verse that could have come straight out of my granny's cottage kitchen in the middle of Offaly's bogs:

> How she'd kiss the cross devoutly when she counted to the end!
> And the visitor would rise at once, and brush his knees – and then
> He'd look very, very foolish as he hit to the boards again.
> She had other prayers to keep him. They were long, long prayers in truth;
> And we used to call them "Trimmin's" in my disrespectful youth.
> She would pray for kith and kin, and all the friends she'd ever known,
> Yes, and everyone of us could boast a "trimmin'" of our own.

Kate's trimmin's were exactly like this and went on for ages. They were longer than the Rosary itself. But everyone and everything got prayed for.

I don't want to give the impression that Kate was a dull "holy Mary" type. Far from it. Kate had her faults. I think she even had her secret faults. But don't we all? She loved her Woodbines and in later years a whiskey and white. She loved Gaelic football and screamed herself hoarse in Croke Park when Offaly played. She kept lodgers and in pre-television days entertained them in the evenings with mock court cases and kitchen boxing competitions. She had a wonderful and mischievous sense of humour.

But to me she was a "living saint". She prayed and she lived and suffered and she prayed. My poor grandfather Paddy was far too fond of the drink and he gave her a hard life. My grandfather spent as much of the weekly wage on drink as he could and that resulted in a great economic struggle for Kate and her three children — Jim (my father), Mary and Tom. Her young son Tom died of heart disease on the kitchen table when he was only eight. Her only daughter Mary also died young of lung disease. Kate had to work all her life to supplement her small income. In 1964 she and I worked in the Gresham Hotel in Dublin together — me as a page boy and she as a kitchen helper.

I know that the vocation that God gave me was recognised by Kate and I know that she prayed secretly for me to be a priest. She was as proud as punch in Holy Trinity Cathedral, Waterford in 1976 when Bishop Michael Russell ordained me a priest. It was an answer to one of her greatest prayers. She was very good to me all the years of my childhood and adolescence and during my time in seminary. She and I went to Rome together in 1971 and attended a public audience with Pope Paul VI. As the Pope was being carried from the audience hall I was at the edge and held up my hand with my breviary in it. I had just finished my first year in seminary. The Pope grabbed my hand tightly and said one word to me: "*coraggio*" — courage. I have always regarded this as Providential — whether the Pope knew it or not himself. God was telling me to have courage for the road ahead. I also feel that it was no coincidence that this event happened with Kate present.

Kate spent the last seven years of her life lying in Blanchardstown Hospital in Dublin, the victim of a stroke. She lost her speech and was semi-paralysed. It was very difficult visiting her and communication was hard. To watch such a live wire laid low like that was tough to cope with. Sometimes I feel guilty that I did not visit her often enough although I did visit regularly. By that time I was living a hundred miles away in Belfast. But her son-in-law, Joe Manning from Banagher, County Offaly, with whom she lived after her daughter Mary died, was exceptionally good to her. And my Dad and Mam visited regularly too.

When Kate died in late 1984 it was I who "said her Mass in black" at Saint Canice's Church, Finglas, Dublin. Incidentally my father Jim, her oldest son, was in the front seat for the funeral. On one occasion I looked down at him and shuddered. I had a premonition that I would be doing his funeral next. Within a few weeks, I had the agonising task of celebrating his funeral Mass at our parish church in Ballygall, Dublin — mid-January 1985.

Kate played a profound part in my spiritual development and in my journey to the priesthood. I know that when she died she went straight to Heaven and that from there she looks after me still.

MY DAD AND MAM WERE VERY DIFFERENT PEOPLE but each complemented the other. I know that they have played a huge part in what I am, both as a human and as a spiritual being.

My Dad, Jim, was born on 6 October 1924 in Tullamore. He was full of the most amazing contradictions and weaknesses but in my heart I feel that he was the very best father that ever walked the earth. I will understand if others make the same claim about their dads.

Dad was very bright at school and was ambitious to do well in life and to raise himself and his family above the alcohol-related hole they were all in. However, at the age of twelve he had to leave school to work, minding cows, so that he could earn a half a crown a week to support the family. Being bright, intelligent and ambitious, his removal from school broke his heart and he secretly resolved some day to catch up on what he had lost.

He later got a job in a textile factory and his intelligence soon saw him rise to the positions of factory supervisor and trade union representative. Very quickly he became a full-time union representative and was appointed Branch Secretary of the Irish Transport and General Workers Union at Carlow. We left Tullamore and moved to Carlow when I was four years old.

His full-time union job came with a car and for the first time we had a family car. Before that, in Tullamore, my father used to ride a bicycle and a motorcycle. The people of Tullamore would smile at the once notorious lad-about-town Jim Buckley as he passed them with me sitting on the bicycle's crossbar or on the motorbike's petrol tank.

We lived in Carlow from 1956 until 1960. I attended primary school with the Mercy Sisters at Carlow. When I wasn't in school I spent my time travelling throughout County Carlow to factories and picket lines and at a very early stage in life learned all about socialism, industrial relations and the championing of the working man and the little man. When I wasn't in school or on my socialist journeys I was helping or doing my homework in the union's branch office sitting at the next desk to my Dad.

When in 1960 Dad was moved to the union headquarters at Liberty Hall, Dublin, I spent many days and evenings in the office of Branch 13, where Dad was first assistant and then Branch Secretary. And I still continued my journeys to factories and places of work and to pickets and was further steeped in the language and strategies of socialism and industrial relations. I know that this early exposure to socialism has had a profound bearing on my thinking ever since. I consider myself left-wing, although not fanatically so. I am a champion of the little man and the black sheep. I am anti-establishment and have a great loathing not for authority, but for authoritarianism.

Eventually Dad decided that it was time for him to catch up on his missed education. He first of all successfully took some A Levels by correspondence from Britain. He then attended University College

Dublin on a part-time basis and received a BA in philosophy, archaeology and economics. He finally spent six or seven years at Dublin's King's Inns and University College Dublin and when he was fifty-seven years old he was called to the Bar as a barrister.

This was a wonderful achievement, and even more so since as well as studying he had to hold down a full-time job to feed his eleven children. He was a man of determination, stubbornness and perseverance. Thanks to him and to God I have inherited those qualities of Jim Buckley's.

When we lived in Carlow Dad brought me to early morning Mass every single day and we lit candles together too. We attended Mass at the Cathedral of the Assumption. It was there too that I received, with my sister Margaret, my First Holy Communion. I loved the Cathedral in Carlow. I loved the stained-glass windows, the smell of incense and candles, the ringing bells, the priest's various coloured vestments. I drank in the whole scene. It all touched and thrilled my soul. More than ever I wanted to be a priest. More than ever I said that I was going to be a priest. Those early morning visits to Mass brought me closer and closer to faith and God and fed my vocation. And my Dad was responsible for that.

But there was another side to Jim. He had a fierce temper and could fly off the handle in an instant and erupt like a volcano. When he was like this, we all cowered. For all his intelligence, he could be very irrational; for some unexplained reason he could also be racist. He hated all Jews because a Jewish moneylender had exploited his mother in her poverty. He suffered greatly from what we today call "road rage" — most other road users were designated illegitimate! He was quite a man for swearing when in a temper and, as they say in County Offaly, "he could make up new ones". He was very tense and took tranquilisers daily in later life. He smoked very heavily — up to eighty cigarettes a day. He developed a heart condition and blocked arteries and died following his seventh or eight heart attack.

On the day he died he seemed to be recovering but as I left at the end of my visit, a look of intense fear came over his face. I realised later that he must have sensed he was going to die.

I got back to Dr Steeven's Hospital while they were still working on him in cardiac care. He was semi-naked and there was blood everywhere. The doctors and nurses thought I was just the hospital chaplain coming to anoint him. I did anoint him and give him general absolution with a very shaky hand and a very choked voice. Then one of the doctors abruptly said "he's gone" and he and I were left alone. I was stunned and stuck to the spot. I just felt numb.

I remember the long walk back down the hospital corridor to the relatives' room where my mother and brothers and sisters were waiting. Still numb, I went through the door and said, "Daddy has just gone to Heaven." The wail of shock and grief that went up will live with me for the rest of my life.

MY MOTHER JO (JOSEPHINE) was the total opposite to my Dad in both personality and temperament. She was born in Tullamore on 27 March 1929. Her father Johnnie Geoghegan was the chauffeur for the Williams family, the famous distillery family of Tullamore. Her mother Margaret was a stay-at-home housewife. My grandfather Johnnie lived into his eighties and married twice, producing some fifteen children with his two wives. My grandmother Margaret, a cigarette smoker, sadly died in her early fifties of throat cancer.

Johnnie was such a good manager of money that you could call him "tight". But he was a great father and husband and a great provider for his family. He also had a dry sense of humour, his tongue like a scalpel. On one occasion when someone was joking him about not being able for a new young wife, he replied, "There's nothing as bad as the sting of a dying wasp." One evening I unexpectedly found myself in Tullamore and knocked on his door around eight o'clock. He came to the door in his pyjamas and said, "I can't let you in now. I'm in bed with my new wife." As a child, I was not sure what to make of that!

My mother appears to have had a very ordinary and normal childhood. She felt loved by her parents and brothers and sisters. Poverty didn't bother them, as my grandfather always brought home plenty of fare from the Williams household.

My mother is an intelligent woman but not overly interested in education, reading or academics. From school, she moved on to a job in Salts textile factory in Tullamore where my dad was a fellow worker and later supervisor. They courted, fell in love and married in July 1951. They lived in various rented flats and houses around Tullamore and, with my mother pregnant and living at home, they struggled financially. I was born in 1952 and we eventually lived in a very decent three-bedroomed council house in Marian Place, Tullamore, until we moved to Carlow.

My mother gave birth to seventeen babies in quick succession — one every eleven or twelve months — an incredible number in today's terms, and quite a lot even then! She coped extremely well with such a large family; she was a natural mother. Sadly she lost six babies at birth or within a short time of birth. All six lost babies were girls. There were three "Marys", one Josephine, a Teresa and an unnamed baby. All were buried in either my grandmother Margaret's grave or in the Angel Plots at Carlow cemetery.

IF MY DAD WAS THE HARD MAN JOHN WAYNE, die-with-your-boots on type my mother was all heart, all emotion and all sensitivity and affection. She lived for her family especially. It was, I think, from her that I got my very sensitive and affectionate nature.

We were quite poor. My father was a very hard worker, sometimes having two jobs. But it was hard for one wage to keep a big family going and both my Mam and Dad smoked. We had lots of debts and creditors always called at the house. I was often despatched to tell them my parents were not at home. I would also be sent with a little money some weeks to creditors or even to county sheriffs to offer a little and beg for clemency. I knew so much about my parents' debts that from the age of nine or ten I would cry about their financial troubles after I went to bed and beg God to help them and take them out of trouble. I knew far too much for a little child.

In some ways, I really had no childhood. Being the eldest of eleven children, I was almost a "third parent". I was only a baby for eleven months when the next one arrived — my sister Margaret. From the day of her birth I stopped being a baby and a child and started my long, long life as a big brother, carer and "parent". There have been many times when it has been a very hard role to fill, as it often means one hundred per cent giving and little or no receiving. But in other ways, today, I am quite comfortable with the parenting, brothering, protecting and helping aspect of my personality. Perhaps it's the ideal personality type for a priest and bishop.

From a very early age I was ready to weep inwardly and outwardly if I saw anyone suffering or in trouble. I would be moved to tears by the sight of a poor woman with children begging on the street. Helping others gave great meaning to my life and really helped me to cope, to believe in myself and to keep going. By the time I was nine or ten years old I was out helping people of all kinds, especially old people and "lame dog" types. I would bring people home to our house for food or shelter or just because they were alone or lonely. I remember once bringing home a prostitute I had met somewhere and giving her tea. After she had left, and Dad heard what her profession was, he made Mam go and wash the toilet she had used with bleach!

Apart from such "informal" ways of helping and "ministering" to others, I had two more "formal" outlets for helping people. Firstly, I joined the Irish Red Cross Society as a uniformed member at the age of fourteen. I trained in first aid and attended football matches, racing events and generally provided first aid cover where crowds gathered. I felt very useful, proud and happy manning ambulances and attending to those who fell ill at such gatherings. I also taught first aid to others. I was very proud of my Red Cross uniform, eventually rising to the dizzy rank of corporal!

I also joined the Legion of Mary, the conservative Catholic organisation devoted to service to God through Mary. The Legion was, and is, dedicated to developing the spiritual lives of its members and those they come in contact with. Later on, as a seminarian and still in the Legion of Mary, I even went on a two-week mission to tenement Glasgow — the Gorbals area — to encourage lapsed Catholics back to Mass and even to convert Protestants to Catholicism. We literally went from door to door peddling conservative devotional Catholicism. Now, all of that seems very embarrassing to me, but that was where I was then.

There was, however, one part of my Legion of Mary work that I am still immensely proud of. The organisation ran two hostels for the homeless in Dublin, the Morning Star Hostel for men and the Regina Coeli (Queen of Heaven) Hostel for women (some of whom were prostitutes). I worked as a volunteer in the Morning Star Hostel making food, serving tables, making beds and generally washing and cleaning. I also spent lots of time listening to the men talking about their lives, their pasts, describing how they had fallen through the fingers of life and ended up on the street. In most cases it had happened through alcoholism. I loved my Morning Star work. It was the real beginning of ministry and priesthood for me.

In another way, it was my "good side" — the opposite of what I thought of then as the "bad side" growing inside me, the side related to my sexuality. I often thought in those times of how the Bible says that a man's good actions make up for his many sins.

Chapter Two

THE WOUNDING

"From that day to this never have my wounds healed"
— Mother Julian of Norwich, fourteenth-century mystic

MY UNWITTING INTRODUCTION to sex occurred when I was sexually abused as a child. I was six. He was eighteen. I was small with tousled hair, bespectacled for a squint and with a front tooth missing. He was tall, blonde and slim. I was a lonely first-born of eleven children, seeking love, attention and affection. He never told me about his feelings or desires.

I have never hated or resented him. I cannot seem to. In a childlike and primitive way, I loved him. And that "love" has never turned to hate. I know now what he did was wrong, I know he wounded me deeply and that I lost my childhood the day he came into my life, yet I find it impossible to view him as an "evil" person.

I cannot remember his name. So I call him Aidan. I like the name Aidan and to this day I feel the need to call my first sexual encounter by a nice name. Aidan used to deliver groceries to our home at Governey Park, Graigcullen in Carlow town. I used to see him coming on one of those great big black messenger bikes with a rectangular frame at the front for holding cardboard boxes full of groceries. He was always the one who brought good things — lemonade and biscuits. I loved my Jacob's Kimberley, Mikado and Coconut Creams. Aidan was like the "Magi" who brought me my "gold, frankincense and myrrh".

My parents got to know Aidan very well and trusted him. He seemed such a lovely young man. Did he deliberately ingratiate himself with my parents? Was it that planned, sophisticated and subtle? My heart hopes not. But I don't know. Eventually Mam and Dad asked him to babysit us once a week while they went to a movie. Aidan agreed.

AIDAN TOOK ME BY THE HAND. I loved him holding my hand. His hand felt so big, so protective, so warm and so comforting. He brought me to our bathroom. He locked the door. I was not afraid. He was my friend. He removed his trousers and went down on his knees. I was amazed at what I saw. His penis was really big, hard and thick. And all that hair! He was rubbing himself and he was getting red, purple. He pulled down my trousers. I was very different from him, small, unaroused, white, hairless. He rubbed me and I did feel a pleasurable tingling. Then I could smell his personal body smell. It was not a bad smell. It was a pleasant, clean and homely smell. Still I was not afraid. A little confused maybe. Here my memories blur. I seem to remember being put astride his large penis but I don't know. I certainly felt a liquid flow and I saw a creamy white substance. Aidan's "crisis" seemed to gradually subside. He looked at me. I cannot remember what was in his look. But it was not frightening. He cleaned me. He cleaned himself. We went to the sitting room where I sat on my friend's knee and had lemonade and biscuits. When my parents came home all seemed normal. It didn't occurred to me to say anything. I was put to bed and got up in the morning for school as normal.

IN UNDERSTANDING AND COMING TO TERMS with my own sexual abuse, I was greatly helped by reading *Secret Life*, the autobiography of the American poet Michael Ryan, who was sexually abused at the age of five. When I read his description of his abuse by a twenty-three-year-old man, something very painful deep inside of me identified with him. Ryan writes:

> The water was warm, the steam rising gently and making the air warm too. Bob said to use both hands, to just put my finger underneath it and tickle it and make it feel good. I started to do what he said and the familiar feeling came back as it stiffened, a dream feel-

ing that before I had had only by myself; it never occurred to me that anyone else ever had it, it seemed naughty, but here was my friend sharing it with me and he didn't think it was bad and we were in this nice secret place together. . . .

. . . he asked me to do the same thing to him. He showed it to me. It was a lot bigger than mine, red and angry. He showed me how to do what he had done; pull my lips over my teeth. He looked like my grandmother when she took out her dentures. . . . It was not long in my mouth the first time, probably less than half a minute before he pulled it out and squeezed it purple in his fist, violently tight, and the cream gushed out.

How many encounters did I have with Aidan? I cannot say. I know that there were several, even many, but somehow my mind seems to have telescoped them all into one bathroom picture.

Years later, when I was in my thirties and trying to cope with my emotions and sexuality, I attended Dr Frank Lake's Primal Therapy course in Nottingham. Apart from mentally revisiting our time in the womb and the moment of our birth we also mentally and emotionally revisited important early happenings in our lives. I "relived" my bathroom experiences with Aidan. By this time I had come to think of what he did to me as abuse. But as I relived the experience, I had to admit to myself that I had experienced some pleasure from my intimate encounters with him. That came as a shock to me, and left me feeling very confused. I cannot explain this. I even feel guilty about writing it here. I'm thinking, "Will other victims of child abuse and anti-abuse campaigners be upset and angry with me for saying this?" The last thing I want to do is to hurt anyone like that. But I must tell the truth as I know it, and perhaps some abuse victims might relate to my experiences in the same way that I related to Michael Ryan's graphic descriptions of the abuse he suffered.

There was one very painful and unpleasant aspect to my relationship with Aidan. Once, he produced a knife and told me he would cut my throat if I ever told anybody about what we did. I was so hurt. I would never let my friend down. How could my friend threaten to kill me with a knife? The threat was a cloud that cast a shadow on my life.

AND THEN THE MOST HURTFUL THING of all happened. Aidan disappeared out of my life, never to be seen again. Suddenly, he was just gone. I was sad and I missed him. As Michael Ryan says: "He was gone, but nothing else changed. If I felt abandoned or betrayed, which I must have, I didn't register it consciously. There was simply a hole in the middle of the world" (*Secret Life*, p. 25).

To this day there is a little corner of my psyche that is still "mourning" for Aidan. I know this must sound strange. But when he went out of my life I missed him in some very primitive but strong fashion. Even today I can find myself subconsciously looking for him. Sometimes if I pass someone in the street who reminds me of him I almost find myself saying, "Is that him?" Or if I am being given change by a shop assistant and a hand accidentally touches mine, I get a start and wonder: "Is that him?" I can't truly explain this. All I can say is that Aidan obviously touched my life at a very profound level. What he did, objectively speaking, was child abuse and paedophilia. But deep within me, Aidan causes unexplained and contradictory feelings, now intimately connected to my emotions and my sexuality. And that at least, I suppose, partly explains why my sexuality is to me and always has been both an agony and an ecstasy.

MENTION THE WORD PAEDOPHILE TODAY and you will most often get an over-the-top, hysterical and totally irrational reaction. Even intelligent and educated people cannot deal rationally with the paedophilia issue. The most common reactions are: "Child abusers should be executed"; "All paedophiles should be castrated"; "They should be thrown into a cell and the keys thrown away"; "They should be burned out" and so on.

Child abuse is one of the most serious evils in our world and one of the most serious crimes anyone can commit. But hysteria and irrationality do not resolve the problem, and in fact can lead to such crazy situations when a consultant paediatrician was burned out of a British housing estate because her ignorant neighbours got the words "paediatrician" and "paedophile" mixed up. We should approach the issue calmly, rationally and intelligently, and we should never forget that people should be presumed innocent until they are convicted.

The jury is really out on the question of whether paedophilia is a learnt response or whether it is genetic. Some experts say that abusers are people who were themselves abused in some way as children. Certainly quite a number of abusers confess that they were abused themselves as children. Perhaps then, certain children who are sexually abused may regard sex between adults and children as something of a "norm". When these abused children grow and become sexually active, they act according to their earlier experiences, if they have not found something to contradict their assumptions. As Dad used to say, "As the twig bends, so the tree grows." In such a sense, could paedophilia be a learnt response and through early experiences that learnt response could be permanently imprinted on the brain and personality?

Other experts say that paedophilia is a sexual orientation that one is born with — an orientation that cannot be changed and that can only be managed. In other words, in the sexual world there are heterosexuals, homosexuals, bisexuals, paedophiles and so on. If paedophilia is something one is born with, that's a very tough call. Imagine being born with a sexual orientation that you can *never* satisfy. It is like asking an alcoholic to stay sober for a lifetime with a pint in his hand, or asking a heroin addict to work in a pharmacy but kick his habit.

I am not saying that the paedophile should ever be allowed to indulge his sexuality. He most certainly should never be allowed to do so. All I'm saying is that to live for a lifetime with the desire for sex with children raging inside you, and never be able to do anything about it, is a hell of a painful life. But I think this must be understood by individuals and by society. No sane person freely decides to be a paedophile. Why would anyone, in their right mind, choose such a painful and obnoxious orientation for themselves? Whatever else it is, paedophilia is a mental disorder, a sickness and an illness. It is, of course, a crime — and should remain one — but it is also an illness.

IN THE COURSE OF MY MINISTRY as a priest and bishop, I have on a couple of occasions had to work with paedophiles. One, "Andrew", who is forty now, is single, says he is gay and suffers with what doctors have called "non-clinical depression". He engages in comfort eating and is hugely overweight as a result. He is neglectful of his appearance, his property and his life in general. He starts new life projects all the time, does no work on them and then drops them. He is lazy, careless, thoughtless and totally uninterested in life. He is very self-centred.

Andrew worked as a social worker in a parish and youth club. He started abusing altar boys and youth club boys when he was eighteen. He sexually abused them in various ways and also beat them with his belt and belt buckle. The authorities say that he even abused children on church pilgrimages to Lourdes in France.

Eventually Andrew was arrested. He protested his innocence. He claimed that he was the victim of a plot by the clergy, teachers and other youth leaders. There were hundreds of charges against him. He got a good barrister and on the day of the trial changed his plea to "guilty" on a few dozen charges, had some others taken into account and got a relatively short sentence as a result. The prosecution and the defence did a deal. Soon after the case one of Andrew's victims committed suicide.

Andrew completed his short sentence and a period on probation. He attended various rehabilitation courses — seldom missing a meeting — but also never really putting his heart into it. He was present only in body but not in spirit. But he kept his slate clean to get through probation. Initially he failed to follow up the possibility of a three-year course in a sexual dysfunction clinic.

Recently Andrew has been exploring whether or not he is gay. He has tried meeting various adults and little or nothing has resulted. Perhaps the real problem is that he is not really gay. Maybe he is hoping he is gay to bring his paedophilia nightmare to an end? Maybe he is paedophile by orientation? A "straight" man cannot become gay. A gay man cannot become "straight" and maybe a paedophile cannot become gay, straight or whatever. Maybe Andrew is trapped within his paedophile orientation.

I do know that Andrew can do much more about managing his difficulty but he seems unwilling. He could be part of a lifetime monthly re-offending prevention meeting. He could go for counselling. He could do his three years of psychosexual therapy. He could force himself to have an interest in life and do things for himself and others. He could exercise and diet. He really needs to take himself by the scruff of the neck and force himself to live an ordered, useful and crime-free life.

But I do not see Andrew living like this. He thinks about the boys he abused and sometimes cries and wants them back. He dreams about them and in his dreams they come to him and forgive him and come back to have a relationship with him. He reminds me of a stout lizard sitting on a rock waiting for its prey — paralysed by the memories of previous prey and by the thoughts and fantasies of future prey.

All the authorities — the police, social services, the probation board and the children's services — regard Andrew as "High Risk": he is in real danger of re-offending. He is in real danger of hurting other children. When I think of Andrew I feel almost a complete hopelessness. He seems impossible to reach.

"JAMES" IS THIRTY-FIVE. When he was thirty, he sexually abused two fourteen-year-olds. James had never had a sexual encounter with another human being until then. The two teenagers discussed sex with him. They talked about masturbation. James exposed himself and them. He masturbated them and then himself. Later the teenagers got some fears and guilt about what had happened and talked to their parents who talked to the police. James was arrested, charged and convicted and received a short prison sentence and a time on probation.

During his prison and probation time he came out as gay. He got help from his GP, his probation officer and a counsellor. He started to visit gay bars and clubs and entered into some relationships. He found his real personal and sexual niche with other adult men. Unlike Andrew, he had never had fantasies about children before his conviction and says he still never has any such fantasies. All his fantasies are about other adult men.

In fact, he is leading a highly promiscuous, cynical gay lifestyle. He finds it hard to let his feelings come into it. He does not even want to know the name of the person he is having sex with. After the sex he likes them to leave immediately or if he is in their place he leaves when the sex is over. If his partner cannot go away James sleeps in the bed and allows the "stranger" to sleep on the floor and depart in the early morning.

James was badly sexually, verbally, mentally and physically abused as a child. He finds it hard to socialise and engage in relationships. He has a lot of mental and psychological baggage. He suffers with depression and is on invalidity and housing benefit. He engages in self-harming by cutting and burning his own body. He drinks heavily and abuses prescribed and illegal drugs. He has taken several overdoses. He says that when he hears his mother is dead he will commit suicide and be buried with her. It is as if he is punishing himself for who he is and what he has done. He says that he can never forgive himself for what he did to the two boys.

Obviously James has a lot of problems and difficulties. But his abuse of the two boys was a one-off. He is not a "paedophile" in the true sense. He was a "situational paedophile" whereas Andrew is a "fixated paedophile". James was a repressed gay man who abused two teenage boys. As an active gay man the likelihood of him re-offending, according to the authorities, is slight or "low risk".

The contrast between these two men illustrates the dangers of the broad brushstrokes with which the media and society paint the problem of paedophilia. There is no one simple solution.

OF COURSE PEOPLE WHO COMMIT SEXUAL CRIMES should have to spend time in detention. And the time spent in detention should reflect the seriousness of the crime they have committed. In general I am in favour of longer than shorter sentences — all of the time of course taking the circumstances into account. And if someone pleads guilty to a crime and saves their victims the trauma of a court case then that plea should be reflected in the sentence. Conversely, I believe that the law needs to deal very firmly with sex offenders who will not submit to therapy and those who are determined to re-offend. In some cases there might be an argument for very long or even permanent detention — for the protection of society and children.

But I do believe that it is not just enough to throw someone into prison and forget about them. While people are undergoing punishment and detention they should also be undergoing intensive group and one-to-one therapy. And when people leave prison they should be obliged by the courts to attend regular re-offending prevention meetings — for life.

I also believe that sex offenders should be segregated from other criminals — murderers and thieves who regard themselves as better than the sex offenders and who generally give the sex offenders a very bad time, often beating them and even raping them. I believe that sex offenders should be held in a specially designed wing or block of their own where the detention/punishment is blended with therapy.

EVEN SEX OFFENDERS ARE HUMAN BEINGS, are they not? Is there not a sense in which when we see or think about a sex offender that we should say: "There but for the grace of God go I"?

We have already accepted that sex offences are serious crimes. We have also accepted that sex offenders should be firmly punished. But rationally and from the Christian perspective especially we must accept that sex offenders, especially those who are trying and determined not to re-offend, need our help and compassion. There is no sin that God cannot and will not forgive — given of course that the sinner is truly sorry and determined (as far as we can all be) not to sin again.

Many sex offenders were sexually abused themselves as children. So there may very well be many cases in which those who perpetrate sex crimes actually began life as victims. Surely that situation calls for compassion?

Of course I am not suggesting that paedophiles are not responsible for their actions. Of course they are and no matter what their sufferings they must take responsibility for themselves and not hurt others, especially children. What I am saying is that a paedophile is responsible for what he does, but may not be responsible for what he is.

So because there may very often be an element of victimhood within the paedophile we must have compassion for him or her. And that compassion must be practical. We must not hate him, though we hate his actions. We must not verbally abuse him. We must not assault him. We must not attack his home or burn him out. And within reason we must allow him to live without social rejection and torture.

There are very real and very serious problems about paedophiles living in housing estates with families or living next to schools. There are problems about paedophiles attending local swimming pools. It is quite right that there be a register of sex offenders and that that register be available to the police and the social services and that these agencies should meet regularly and monitor all offenders on the register. But I do not agree that such registers should be made totally public. What right do a gang of vigilantes have to go to the local library, pick out someone from the register and go on a head-bashing expedition?

I think that it is better for paedophiles themselves if they can live in non-estate locations — say in apartments or flats in a commercial or industrial area. They are more likely to be allowed to live in peace there. In fact perhaps the best place for convicted sex offenders would be a community setting — the equivalent of the sheltered dwelling idea for the elderly. Many paedophiles are very lonely. They have been rejected by family and friends. Loneliness can sometimes make people re-offend. Would it not be better if the government sponsored sheltered dwelling communities, away from family estates?

GOD LOVES PAEDOPHILES AS MUCH as he loves everyone else! He "hates" what paedophiles do. But He loves the *people* who happen to be paedophiles.

Paedophiles and sex offenders are today's "lepers". If we are Christian we have to approach these modern lepers with the same love and compassion Jesus showed the lepers of his day. One leper said to Jesus: "Sir, if you want to you can cure me." Jesus answered: "Of course I want to. Be cleansed." Of course Jesus often told people to go away and not sin again. So to the sex offender and the paedophile we too must say: "Go and do not sin again." But we must also find a way to make the modern lepers loved, accepted and cleansed. We must especially try to find a way to help them to live with their condition and to manage it so that they hurt no-one, especially children, and not even themselves.

As Christians we believe that God loves all men and women equally and that we can never do anything that makes God stop loving us. But we also believe as Christians that our bodies are the "temple of the Holy Spirit" and that God expects us not to sully that temple by hurting either God Himself or by hurting any of our brothers and sisters. So we can always say that God loves the sinner but not the sin.

And we know from Jesus that God has a very special love for little children. At one stage in the ministry of Jesus the disciples tried to stop little children approaching Christ and He became very indignant with His disciples. He said: "Let the little children come to me; for it is to such as these that the Kingdom of God belongs." Christ was also very severe on anyone who ever hurt a child. Of those who hurt children Christ said: "It would be better for a man to have a stone tied around his neck and be thrown into the sea than for him to hurt one of these, my little ones." In the eyes of God a sin against a little child is one of the most serious sins that anyone can ever commit. So paedophiles, when they hurt children, commit, from the Christian perspective, one of the greatest sins that men and women are capable of committing.

As Christians, among our core beliefs is that we will appear before God for judgement and depending on the outcome of that judgement we pass either into eternal happiness (heaven) or eternal unhappiness (hell). So the paedophile, like all of us, will appear before God to be judged. God tells us in the Bible that He will judge us, not by externals, but by what He finds in our hearts. We will not be able to fool or manipulate God. So like the rest of us the paedophile will have his or her heart thoroughly examined by God. So the paedophile, like us all, will need a pure heart.

We know that God is a just judge. In earthly courts, we most often get "law" and not true justice. But God will not only give us pure justice. He will give us the purest of justice — Divine Justice. True justice takes every circumstance into account. And when judging all of us, including paedophiles, God will take everything into account — our genes, our childhood, any damage or abuse we suffered and each and every circumstance of our life. God's justice will take into account every single thing that ever happened us. In that sense God will judge us absolutely fairly and our "sentence" will be built upon and reflect all the influences that shaped our lives.

Finally we must know that if we want God to forgive us absolutely for our sins we must be "truly sorry" for them. And that means that we fully acknowledge what we did was evil; we did it knowing that it was evil, that we regret what we did and that we were absolutely determined never to do it again. If the paedophile feels like this about his/her paedophilia God will forgive him/her their paedophile thoughts, actions and sins.

I can acknowledge that some people will find it hard to believe that God will forgive a paedophile and let him/her into heaven. Victims of paedophilia will especially find this notion very painful. I am very sorry about that pain. But we Christians believe that there is no sin that God will not and cannot forgive once the sinner is truly sorry. We cannot exclude paedophiles from God's boundless forgiveness just to be politically correct.

Meditating on the question of God forgiving a paedophile in March 2003 I found myself penning the following verse based on the ancient Christian and indeed biblical story of the forgiveness of Dismas, the "Good Thief" at the eleventh hour:

The Good Paedophile

I am Dismas, the "Good Thief".
At twelve noon the sky turned strangely dark.
I would be hanging on my cross for hours.
Hands and legs bound by coarse ropes.

I was here to die for my heinous crimes.
I deserved what was happening.
My executioner was thirst, wounds and hunger;
A well-deserved slow death in the noonday sun.

Twelve feet away another prisoner swore and writhed,
Cursing God and man and mocking his victims.
Impenitent and without fear of judgement;
A man who had lost all sense of right and wrong.

Suddenly I saw a Man as bright as the Sun!
He was stripped and pegged to a rough cross too.
Then they placed him between us two;
He was nailed as well as roped!

The unrepentant jeered at him.
Taking up the chorus of the rabid crowd.
But looking on his wounds I was strangely moved,
A cerebral whisper said: "Your God! Your God!"

I found myself addressing this fallen God.
I told him all I'd thought and done.
He wept when I told him of the children I'd hurt,
The details made him scream with grief.

Through blood, sweat and tears he coughed:
"Better a man bound with stone drown in the sea
Rather than he hurt one of my little ones."
I said: "I've scraped the bottom of my human barrel."

He sobbed for the innocence I had debauched.
He made me wish I had died at birth.
Then the weak spark of goodness in me screamed:
"Jesus, remember me when you come into your kingdom."

First I beheld the little faces I had ravaged;
A wicked sea of gory black and red.
But then! I saw the Throne of Mercy rise;
And at God's feet I saw despair give birth to hope!

Dying, I hear: "Today you will be with me in Paradise."

My early sexual experience was certainly a serious wounding. Ever since, if not before, I have been wounded at the sexual level. As a Christian, God's place in all of this is important to me. This brings me up against old questions, questions like: "Why does God allow bad things to happen to innocent people — especially to children?"

God Himself of course does not do bad things to people and I know that He would abhor any kind of abuse of children. But He does allow bad things to happen, even to children; things like cancer, HIV, abuse and even murder. Why? In this dilemma I have never found simple answers but I have been helped by the kind of thought conveyed in this short verse I once discovered:

> Good forever on the scaffold;
> Evil always on the throne;
> But God stands within the shadows;
> Keeping watch upon His own.

It is not really what happens to one in life that is important. Rather, it is how one handles what happens. Some people allow their life sufferings to make them bitter and resentful. Bitterness and resentment are cancers of the heart. They hurt the person who feels them more than they hurt the person against whom these feelings are directed. So when we suffer we should try to tackle our suffering. If a problem can be solved we should solve it. But there are some sufferings and troubles that cannot be solved and we must live with these things. Further, not only must we live with them, we must transform them and use them to make us better people.

God allowed me to be sexually abused when I was six. I do not know why He allowed that. But He did. That abuse was a serious wounding and has affected my life greatly. It has caused me a lot of pain and suffering. I can spend my life being bitter, resentful, angry and depressed about that abuse. Or I can get on with my life. And is it not possible that certain qualities have grown out of my suffering? Perhaps some aspects of my faith, maturity and compassion are somehow the product of my sufferings, especially my sexual abuse?

The Wounding

HOW HAVE I BEEN WOUNDED? How do I experience my wound? Well obviously I was wounded at the level of my sexuality. It is wounding and damaging for a small boy to have a sexual encounter with an adult man. I think that psychology and psychiatry still have a great deal to learn from and teach the rest of us about how deeply damaging such encounters are.

Did that early childhood experience make me homosexual? I don't know. I do know that some uncles of my mother were "closeted" homosexuals. If I had some homosexual genetic material in me, did my sexual abuse consolidate those leanings? I don't know.

I do know that all my life I have suffered feelings of ugliness, unworthiness, uncleanliness, inferiority, fear, insecurity, panic, embarrassment, self-consciousness, and I know that there is at least some connection between all these painful negative emotions and the fact that I was sexually abused as a child.

Aidan was my abuser, but he was also my first intimate friend and contact with another non-family human being. For some reason I formed a major emotional attachment to him and his departure, in some way I cannot properly explain, emotionally blew me out of the water. Whatever capacity for loneliness existed in me before I met him, before he abused me, after his departure my loneliness became a chasm that with the passage of time and so many other complications took on emotional "Grand Canyon" proportions. My primary wound in life, if not my aboriginal wound, is loneliness! A lot of the time I feel very lonely, almost hopelessly so, but never, thank God, suicidally lonely.

Of course because of my faith I agree with the great St Augustine: "Our hearts were made for you O Lord and we shall find no rest until we rest in Thee." I know and believe that I will only find my ultimate happiness with God in Paradise — whatever that paradise is. But I am human, very human, and of late I ask God everyday to give me the gift of a companion in this life. I leave this request at God's feet every morning and hope He will be generous enough to answer my human prayer and need.

However the worst thing anyone can believe is that their wounds and sufferings do not have meaning. They do. When God wounds us it is always, always a healing wound. We cannot always feel this. The hand that hurts is the hand that heals. My woundedness has tempered my pride and made me rely heavily of God and faith. My woundedness has also made me compassionate to others. My woundedness is intimately connected to my call as priest.

For so much of my life I "justified" my existence (and I suppose made up for my sins) by *doing* — always doing good deeds for others, things that made me feel I was a good person and not a bad person. But in the past number of years I have learned one of life's great lessons — that it is more important *"to be"* than it is *"to do"*. And I've also learned that if I give away one hundred per cent of myself every day I will soon become exhausted and burnt out. So through pain and counselling I have learned to give fifty per cent and take fifty per cent. In other words I have learned to look after myself as well as others. I have also learned that if I look after myself I will be so much more settled and regularly renewed within myself as to be able to give even more to others.

AT A VERY EARLY AGE, two powerful human phenomena had met in me. My great childhood loneliness met with, and in some way connected with, the whole area of sexuality, so brutally introduced into my life at a much too early age. As I look back on my childhood — quite calmly and dispassionately — I can see these two milestones. And as I grew older I had these two very heavy bags to drag along behind me, bags I could never seem to let go of — a bag of loneliness and a bag of sexual abuse.

Where did or does God and spirituality come into all this? Even as a child I got great comfort in every part of my life from praying, going to Mass, lighting candles and, from the age of three, wanting to be a priest. In His own way I firmly believe that God was walking with me and watching over me. He didn't stop bad things happening to me. But I don't blame Him for that and I have no problem with it.

Much worse things happened and happen to other little children and God does not step in and prevent it all. But I believe that He was with me and watching over me and in some strange way was allowing me to become the person He wanted me to be by allowing me to have all the experiences, good and bad, that He allowed me to have.

I've often heard it said that the earlier a child learns to play a musical instrument, the greater a musician the child will become. Perhaps it is the same with the art of discipleship? Maybe the earlier one is exposed to the "slings and arrows", the greater becomes the capacity for faith and compassionate ministry?

Chapter Three

AN AGONISING PUBERTY: LONELINESS, SEXUALITY, SPIRITUALITY

"He struggles like a butterfly which is pinned alive into an album. But through all the horror he can continue to want to love."
— Simone Weil, The Love of God and Affliction

"Pray that your loneliness may spur you into finding something to live for, great enough to die for". — Dag Hammarskjöld

AS A TEENAGER, I FELT even more alone in the world. I had few or no friends of my own age. I did not play sports, go to the cinema or discos or any of the other things my peers were doing. And I was, more than ever, a third parent in the home — still doing housework, shopping and child minding.

I can remember long Sunday afternoons when my parents rested and it was my job to keep all the younger children out of the house for hours and hours. I herded them around Glasnevin in Dublin — up and down streets, through town parks and Glasnevin cemetery from lunchtime until teatime. My younger brothers and sisters still talk about these pilgrimages in pleasant terms, jokingly calling me the cruel and bullying big brother.

But they didn't realise then that while their "cruel" shepherd, under strict parental instructions, was herding them around the roads of north Dublin he was present to them in body only. For he was really lost in a melancholic day dream and trance in which a great storm was raging and the waves of an indescribable loneliness were crashing on his emotional shoreline.

I was lonely. I was falling in love and getting crushes. I was having "bad thoughts" and "bad actions" with myself and feeling guilty and repressed and running to confession. I was praying and going to church and wanting to be a priest.

I was in great inner turmoil. But again thoughts of God and my faith and religious practice and thoughts of priesthood were hugely comforting.

THE FIRST PRIEST I EVER REALLY KNEW WELL was Fr John Hyde, a Jesuit Professor of Theology at Milltown Park but also a hugely pastoral and holy priest with the gift of healing. Father Hyde used to visit my childhood home, talk to me and give me the tops of his two boiled eggs. My admiration for him played a not insignificant part in me wanting to be a priest. Fr Hyde was the sort of man from whom you could benefit spiritually just by being in his company. It would not be possible to spend any length of time with him without some of his holiness and spirituality rubbing off on you. My grandmother had such faith in him that, without his knowledge, she would put his hat on her head to ward off headaches and drink the tea he left in his tea cup as if it were holy water! He was also a very shy, humble man. In the Order he was so quiet and modest that his nickname was "Hyde and seek".

Later in life, I occasionally went to confession to Fr Hyde. I never discussed my sexuality with him. I'm sure he would not have had a problem with it but I felt that he was so holy and pure himself that I would shock him. I'm sure he would be a little perturbed at my ecclesiastical disobedience. But I know that I benefited hugely spiritually by knowing Fr Hyde and having occasional contact with him for the first thirty years of my life. I concelebrated his funeral Mass at Gardiner Street Jesuit Church in Dublin.

MY SEXUALITY, FOR MOST OF MY LIFE, was the principal source of pain and inner anguish in my life, at least until I was in my early forties. First of all there was the "loss" of my "relationship" with my abuser — a strange loss. But every loss is painful and especially so to a child. Then there was the guilt that I took on for what had happened. Even though I was a totally innocent victim I took on the guilt of the episode, as is common to many abused children. Little children think that adults are great and good and it's the children who are bold and naughty. If something bold and naughty had happened — and it must have done because my "friend" left me and loved me no more — then surely I had done something awfully wrong? It had to be my fault!

Then of course as the years went on and at the beginning of puberty I became conscious of being sexually different — I liked boys instead of girls — the whole thing became compounded.

From the time therefore that I was a little child I felt "different" and "alienated" from others — especially my peer group. I had the loneliness of the oldest child. I had had my sexual abuse. I had lost my "friend" over what I did. And I sexually fancied other boys.

As a kid I was also chubby and I was often called names like "fatso". From the very beginning I saw myself, and was taught to see myself, as ugly, dirty and absolutely unworthy in God's eyes. So my inner ugliness was reflected in my outer ugliness. As a child and adolescent I felt unattractive, unlovable and very, very lonely.

It was at that early stage that I first learned to identify with the alienated, outcast Christ, Himself the friend of the alienated and outcast. I'm sure my present day love of the spirituality of the alienated must have had its roots in the little lonely, sexually abused, different, ugly duckling child.

I never would have dreamed of blaming God for my misfortunes. If adults were "good" then God was "perfectly good" and I was a rotten little sinner. In school I learned all about sins — mortal, which led to the total death of the relationship with God; and venial, which left the soul black and dirty and needing cleaning.

There was only one hope for me. Jesus had saved the world through suffering. Suffering, I thought, was the currency God liked best. If I suffered and offered up my suffering to God with Christ on the Cross then God might take pity on me and save me. I was so convinced of this that my primary prayer, after the Mass which was the re-enactment of Christ's suffering, was to perform the Stations of the Cross, following the different stages of Christ's suffering on His path from Jerusalem to Calvary. At each station I reminded myself that Christ went through this for my sins and I found some suffering in my life to identify with Christ at each of the fourteen stations. He received his cross; I received my sexuality as my cross. He was tortured by the soldiers, the agents of the Devil; I was tortured by my "impure thoughts", also the agents of the Devil. Jesus fell three times; I fell every time I masturbated or had a sinful thought. And on and on my daily childhood journey went as I made my way to God and to the priesthood.

My childhood God was a God who loved me but was also a God who saw me doing bad things and being a bad person, a God who was detective, prosecutor, judge, jury and jailor. For that God I had to run to confession very often and beg forgiveness, do much penance and make much sacrifice.

And I dreamed of priesthood. If I became a priest I would have achieved victory over my body, my sexuality and the world and I would also spend my life serving God. That would surely please Him and get me into Heaven.

Today, twenty-nine years after ordination and thirty-five years after entering the seminary, I thank God and destiny that I am a priest. But my idea of God and my idea of priesthood and prayer could not be more different than it was when I was a struggling little soul.

I CANNOT UNDERSTAND HOW I got through puberty and my teens without at least having a serious nervous breakdown. Only two things saved me — and in this order — my passionate craving to be a priest and daily belief in and prayer to God. I am not being pious or precious when I say this. It was not like that. I went through years of absolute mental torture during which I felt I was holding onto life and sanity by my fingernails.

Between the ages of six and twelve, I had not thought much about sex or what Aidan had done to me. Like all kids of that age I did engage occasionally in "playing mammies and daddies" in the garden shed with other children when we would say to each other "you show me your bum and I'll show you mine." I was also very close to my sister Margaret. We would lie on a bed, tickle each other's backs and arms with our fingers and occasionally with a soft hair brush — all totally normal and harmless.

Then twelve and thirteen came and with it came the explosion of hormones and bodily changes. My first moment of harmless but noticeable excitement came when a neighbour, a boy my own age, invited me to his room. We decided to play doctors. He lay on his bed face down, pulled down his pants and invited me to give him an imaginary injection. The sight, the experience, the faint pleasant smell and the forbidden patch of human skin excited me. Absolutely nothing happened. But it stuck in my mind. I would have liked if we had played doctors more often! But we never did.

Sometime later I discovered masturbation. I found it at the beginning to be both pleasurable and confusing. There was also an element of pleasant pain as one's body adjusted. Of course I also knew it was a very great "mortal sin". But that never stopped it happening. Instead, I went to confession each time it happened and before going to Holy Communion. I got some awful telling-offs in confession. I was convinced beyond doubt that one act of masturbation would lead to eternal damnation if I didn't confess.

With puberty and masturbation came the fantasies. I knew them then as "impure thoughts" and not as fantasies. The fantasies were very rarely about girls or women; generally they involved males. The word "gay" was not really in vogue at the time. I knew words like "homosexual", "queer", etc., but could never have allowed myself to put any tag on myself. I just confessed "bad thoughts and impure actions with myself".

With the fantasies came the memories of Aidan and with my developing "morality" came a guilt about what had happened with Aidan. I applied all that guilt to me and none to Aidan. By now I had a dark secret. Whatever happened to me, I felt I must never tell anyone about what happened with Aidan and me. I must never tell anyone, outside of confession, about my bad thoughts and actions. Even in confession, I could not tell the nature of my thoughts. I had a dark sexual secret and I had to strive with all my energy never, ever, to let anyone find out about me.

That was hard. Because whenever sex was mentioned anywhere, I blushed to the roots. I was convinced that everyone could see me blushing and that I was giving away the fact that I had a dark sexual secret. That made me blush all the more. There was nothing I could do about it. I was in perpetual agony.

All of this led to major problems relating to my peer group. I did not have any friends at home. I had few friends in school. I was terrified that these other boys would find out about Aidan and about my bad thoughts and actions. I was sexually attracted to some of my classmates and this made it all so much worse. I longed to bond with some of them but feared them finding out about me. I was in total turmoil.

So what could I do? I had to opt out. I had to get away from these peers that both attracted and threatened me. So I refused to go to school.

My Dad, who had been unjustly deprived of an education, saw education as the number one thing he wanted for his children. He thought that I was just spoiled or lazy or bold. He physically dragged me every morning into the car. He physically dragged me into the school, the classroom and the bench. He stood over me, as all my classmates watched, until the teacher arrived, and then he left. I always ran out of the room, or got out the window, or escaped from the car and ran home. At lunchtime I faced his wrath. The same scenario was repeated on many mornings and afternoons. Eventually I was totally distressed. He gave up!

I WAS BROUGHT TO OUR LOCAL GP in Glasnevin/Ballymun, Dr Brian Daly of Griffith Avenue. Dr Daly was a lovely, kind man and a very thorough doctor, but there was nothing he could do for me. He referred me to the Child Guidance Clinic at Dublin's Mater Hospital. Here I met another fine doctor and beautiful man — Dr Paul McQuaid, the nephew of the famous, or infamous, Archbishop of Dublin, Dr John Charles McQuaid. Dr McQuaid worked hard with me. He talked to me. He listened. He got me to do drawings. He even brought me for drives in his car to observe me. He would drive to my school and observe my reactions as we got near the school.

At times he ventured near to discussing the emotional and sexual. When he did this, I always ended the session by crying. I was not able to discuss my dark secret with him. I regret that now. How wonderful it would have been to unburden myself at twelve or thirteen years of age. But I was too afraid, too guilty. I was too young to cope with opening up to him. When I went to Dr McQuaid I was really struggling with puberty, my sexual awakening, my dawning homosexuality and the whole question of having being sexually abused. How could I have been expected to handle such major issues, even with help, at thirteen years of age? He did his very best for me but I wasn't ready. My life may have been very different if I had let go and let Dr McQuaid untangle my very tangled ball of wool. However, I believe there is a destiny to these things. I'm not sure I would have wanted my life to be different.

In frustration, Dr McQuaid admitted me to hospital for six weeks. He would see me twice a day. But he made no progress. I enjoyed my time in hospital. I was housed as a semi-private patient in St Vincent's ward of the Mater Hospital. (I was actually a patient in the Mater the night the IRA blew up Nelson's Pillar. I heard the bang during the night and the next day I went down and took a piece of the rubble as a souvenir.) I loved the ward sister and all the nurses. I helped the staff with bed-making and the care of the older patients. I even sat with old people as they died. I visited home lots of days — as if I was visiting from some prestigious college. But I was determined. I was not going to let Dr McQuaid get hold of my dark secret. Pat was coping well — except when anyone came near addressing his dark secret. My distress only intensified.

I HAD A LOVELY REUNION with Dr Paul McQuaid in December 2004, thirty-seven years after I had last seen him in the Child Guidance Clinic. Carry Crowley of RTE Radio 1 had broadcast one of her *Snapshots* programmes with me in the interviewee's chair. During the programme I had mentioned my sexual abuse and had also mentioned Dr Paul McQuaid. Dr McQuaid contacted RTE for a copy of the interview and he also contacted me. We corresponded and eventually met for lunch. We had an animated chat for two and a half hours and have agreed to meet again.

At our December 2004 meeting I was able to tell Paul all the things that I had been unable to tell him nearly four decades earlier — about my abuse, my homosexuality and even about how I had had a secret mad crush on him. (When I first met Paul McQuaid he was only twenty-nine or thirty years old. He was tall, dark-haired and extremely handsome. All the nurses in the hospital were "dying stone dead" about him, as we say in Ireland.) Paul told me that he had never been able to work out what was wrong with me. It was a mystery to him. Of course, back in the mid-1960s none of the professions were truly aware of the extent of child abuse in Ireland.

THE OUTCOME OF THE CHILD GUIDANCE CLINIC experience was that my Dad accepted that I was not going to go to school. But he said: "You are not going to idle at home. You'll have to get a job." I did.

My first job was as a lift operator in O'Reilly's department store in Dublin's Earl Street. I enjoyed this job. Operating a lift gave me "authority" and "status" and was the next best thing to driving a car! I don't know how many times customers said the line, "I imagine this job has its ups and downs!" My only problem in the lift job was an old lady who worked at the top of the store. She had some sort of hygiene problem. She would get into the lift to be taken to the top and her awful personal smell would linger. People getting into the lift would look at me accusingly. I used to take the lift to the basement and spray it with air freshener. I spent a lot of my £3 per week on air freshener!

From the lift I progressed to CIE, the public transport company, as a messenger. My boss, a married man, specialised in cornering young boys in the stationery store and fondling them. Someone warned me and I avoided him. In 1966/67, my wages were £4.6s.0p. I spent a year in the job. I felt like a private detective flashing my bus pass on Dublin's buses. When I turned sixteen, I had to pay tax and social insurance, and my wages dropped from £4.6s.0p to £3.19.0p. But I was still happy with the status which flashing the bus pass conferred on me. I also liked the uniform!

At the time CIE had a policy of sending their young employees to school by "day release". At sixteen, I returned to school for two half days a week. I was sent to the College of Commerce in Rathmines. I loved it. It was so unlike the Christian Brothers and priest-run secondary schools I had tried and failed to attend. In Rathmines there was no corporal punishment. If you worked they encouraged you. If you didn't they ignored you. I thrived in this free environment and worked hard. I passed my end-of-year examination — the Group Certificate. I then decided to leave work and return to school full-time. I still wanted to be a priest and realised that I needed my Leaving Certificate.

After school at four o'clock I would go to my Dad's office at Liberty Hall where he was a trade union official. We would have our tea at five o'clock and then he and I would go to the National Library in Kildare Street. We would study from six until ten at night. At the time he was studying for an arts degree in philosophy, archaeology and economics, which he passed. Later he studied law for six years and was called to the bar at fifty-seven years of age. I had some very good teachers in the College of Commerce, and with all the hard study, I got my Leaving Cert in the year.

The College of Commerce was not without a "gay challenge" for me. One of our teachers, a man in his forties, was obviously gay. He used to go around the class, leaning over students to examine their work. He would stroke them and hug them from behind. On one occasion he asked me to help him bring a group of disadvantaged children from Dublin on a bus trip to England. I gladly obliged. On the first night we were in England, the kids were settled and I was sitting in the teacher's room. He asked me to get into my pyjamas and get into bed beside him. I sat on his bed and talked to him. I was not attracted to him and even if I was, my "morality" then would not have allowed me to do such a thing — and I wanted to be a priest. I told him all of this. I said, "I know you are more than forty and I am only eighteen. I know that you are a teacher and I am a pupil. I know that you are lonely and I feel for you in that. I cannot do what you want but I do want to be a comforting friend to you." He got angry and said, "If you will not come to bed, then go away." I was sad. Our friendship ended. I do not know what has happened him since. I hope that he did not suffer too much. When I think of people like him I think of the words of Henry David Thoreau, "Most men live lives of quiet desperation."

WHEN I WAS IN MY TEENS and living in Ballygall, North Dublin, we had three wonderful priests in our parish. The parish priest was Fr John Pierce who later became Canon Pierce and the parish priest of Rathmines. The two curates were Fr Joe Collins, a Kerry man and Fr Michael Lambe. I was deeply impressed by all three wonderful priests and wanted to be a good priest like them.

I admired Fr Joe Collins for his wonderfully practical sermons, for his twenty-four-hour dedication to his parishioners and for the simplicity of his life — reflected in the "banger" of a car he drove! I used Fr Joe a lot as a confessor. But I became closest of all to John Pierce, the parish priest. He was a tall, dignified white-haired man who dressed both immaculately and grandly. He always wore a perfectly fitting black suit and collar and when outdoors wore a grand crombie overcoat, accompanied by black leather gloves and an

Anthony Eden formal hat. His Roman cassock was also perfectly tailored. He also drove, in his sixties and seventies, a Triumph Herald sports car — just like the one Dr Paul McQuaid drove.

When John Pierce found out that I wanted to be a priest he took me under his wing. He gave me a little extra pocket money and brought me regularly to the cinema and to a posh restaurant afterwards for high tea. I can remember some embarrassing moments in cinemas; if a couple on the screen went any further than a brief kiss, Canon Pierce would loudly announce, "Right Pat, let's go. I'm not standing for any of this." He would storm out of the auditorium followed by my good self. In the cinema lobby he would ask to see the manager and make a formal complaint about the "impurity" on the screen.

Canon Pierce was also Archbishop John Charles McQuaid's apostle to Dublin's female and male prostitutes. With the help of a special branch of the Legion of Mary, Canon Pierce used to walk the streets at night, approaching prostitutes as they worked and asking them to stop working and come with him to a Legion of Mary premises where they got tea and counselling. Most of the girls took the tea but didn't stop working. But I often passed these girls in Dublin with Canon Pierce and they also gave him a great and fond wave. He always whispered to me under his breath, with the look of a KGB man on his face, "Pat, they are some of my ladies".

I loved Canon Pierce for his great clerical dress sense, his innocence and simplicity and his utter devotion to his priesthood. Even though he never gave me the slightest reason to believe so I always suspected that with his fussiness and quasi-effeminacy he himself was gay. If he was I doubt he ever did anything about it, which must have caused him much inner pain. In fact, "gay" would be a crude word in Canon Pierce's case; in recognition of his dignity I should say that he was "of the antique disposition"!

There were and are many other good priests whom I have met throughout my life whom I have admired and from whom I have benefited greatly spiritually and in many other ways: Fr Tom "Tommo" O'Flynn (RIP), Vincentian Father and spiritual director of

Clonliffe seminary; Dr Tony Hayes (RIP), Rosminian Father, my confessor at St John's in Waterford; Monsignor John Shine, the President of St John's, who took me under his wing after I was expelled from Clonliffe; Fr Andrew Burns, Paraclete Father, of Gloucestershire who was my confessor and who kept me sane when I was in Wales; Monsignor Patrick Mullally (RIP), who was a real hierarchical bully but who accepted me into Down and Connor diocese and who had a sneaking regard for the rebel in me; Canon Walter Larkin (RIP), my parish priest in Kilkeel who was feared by all his curates but who was very kind to me; Fr Paddy McVeigh, my parish priest in Larne when Cahal Daly sacked me in 1986 and who said at the time: "I wish I had your balls"; Fr Michael Keane, founder of the Knock Marriage Bureau who was done a grave injustice by the then archbishops of Tuam and Dublin because he wanted to bring some accountability and democracy into church structures; and Fr Des Wilson, the Belfast-based human rights campaigner who was unjustly sacked from his parish by Bishop William Philbin of Belfast. From all of these men, to a greater or lesser degree, I received kindness, understanding and inspiration. And through them I learned important life and spiritual lessons.

I EXPERIENCED SOMETHING ELSE during my adolescence that I thought was peculiar to me but that I have since learned, through reading and talking to others, is quite common. I experienced the anxiety that my father might castrate me! I can remember being in our upstairs bathroom at home in Ballymun one evening. I think I may have been there to sexually relieve myself. As I opened the bathroom door I saw my father coming up the stairs. I immediately closed and locked the door, filled with the irrational fear that my Dad was actually coming up the stairs with a knife to do the job. In hindsight I know how ridiculous this may sound, but at the time it was so real and filled me with such terror. I know from my work and ministry that many have had similar "irrational" but normal and common fears.

During puberty I "fell in love" often, but only from a distance, and I could never articulate the feelings. I remember seeing an attractive, needy and possibly gay young man in a church, longing to bond with him but doing nothing about it except feeling intensely lonely and empty. In puberty I couldn't even articulate these things to myself, much less to others. Many years later, however, I was able to write a poem about him:

A Stranger

The stranger passed,
Knelt, began to pray.
A face was pale,
A body tense.
From head to foot
An aura of emptiness,
Boredom, loneliness, and insecurity.
There was also hope, searching,
And a desire to be touched and reached.
I was alerted and deeply moved.
Everything in me
Was reaching out,
No — crying out.
Seeking to comfort and to touch.
Wanting to show
Understanding and care.
The tender possibilities excited.
Too quickly prayers ended.
My stranger stood, and passed.
Eyes met.
Hearts understood.
Nature's found recognition.
But inhibition won.
Sadness enveloped me.
The panic of lost opportunity.
And then another haunting thought.
Was it I who needed, desired,
And didn't receive?
Had selfishness been denied?
Or had a beautiful,
Never to be regained opportunity,

> Passed through my trembling fingers;
> Filled as they were
> With the fear of being wrong,
> Rejected?
> And at last
> The saddest thought: That,
> I, would never know!

Another distant unknowing love was a young student doctor who was a member of the Red Cross with me. I cried in bed about these "loves" and masturbated about them and later confessed my bad thoughts and actions. But I had no sexual experiences whatsoever. I wanted to be a priest. I wanted to be pure. And as the Church taught me at the time, everything sexual was a sin. I was committing the lesser mortal sin — with myself.

I cannot find the words to convey how lonely I was during these years. I continued to go to church every day and do the Stations of the Cross. My loneliness and sexual frustration were my Calvary, my Cross. I offered up my sufferings with the sufferings of Christ as the Church had taught me. I don't know if I could make it through those years again. Thank God I don't have to.

Chapter Four

SEX IN THE SEMINARY

"Well, we all get by Fathers, don't we, on the three excesses: excessive whiskey, excessive golf and excessive masturbation" — A priest retreat master to one hundred Dublin priests during a recent retreat

I ENTERED THE SEMINARY AT EIGHTEEN and was ordained when I was twenty-four. At twenty-four, when I knew nothing, but thought I knew everything, the Catholic Church forced me to take a promise of celibacy — not a vow of celibacy, as secular priests outside religious orders do not take vows. But they would not have ordained me if I did not promise to be celibate and anyway I was so idealistic and naïve at that age that I would have said or done nearly anything they told me to do.

How can the Catholic Church ask such a young person to commit themselves to a totally "unnatural" life? How can the Catholic Church bind people to compulsory celibacy when the Lord Himself did not request or demand it and when in its traditions the Church had married priests and bishops right into the early Middle Ages?

How could a semi-brainwashed, repressed, closeted and totally inexperienced twenty-four-year-old have known what was involved in lifelong celibacy? How could such a person know about the cold breezes of loneliness that blow and chill to the bone in the thirties, forties, fifties, sixties and seventies? I don't feel at all morally bound by a "promise" I had no freedom but to take and a promise made in immaturity, naïveté and ignorance.

I believe very strongly in optional celibacy for priests or indeed for anybody who has that charism, that call. I know some wonderful, truly celibate priests and lay people whose self-imposed celibacy makes them wonderful servants of God and others. But you cannot impose celibacy. You cannot turn a charism into a law. Celibacy is for the chosen few. For the rest of us, priests or lay people, "it is not good for a man (or a woman) to be alone".

I ATTENDED TWO SEMINARIES, firstly Holy Cross College, Clonliffe, Dublin, and secondly St John's College in Waterford. Homosexual activity was prevalent in both seminaries, as indeed it is in all seminaries. In my own experience homosexuality was more prevalent in Clonliffe than it was in St John's. I had no sexual experience in either college; not because I didn't desire to — I did — but because I was very repressed and was convinced it was a mortal sin. I also passionately wanted to be a priest and did not want to get expelled.

I entered the seminary for the Archdiocese of Dublin — Holy Cross College, Clonliffe — in September 1970, and very soon discovered that at least some, if not many, seminarians were having sex with each other. This "problem" had, presumably, been going on for some time, as there were strict restrictions on students entering each other's rooms and also strict restrictions on younger and older seminarians mixing too much. For instance in my time in Clonliffe you were not allowed out of your room after eleven o'clock at night to go to the toilet. Each student was supplied with a ceramic pot in which to "do his business". I imagine that this rule was introduced to counteract the excuse that students moving about at night were travelling to and from the toilet when in fact they were travelling to and from each other.

Clonliffe College officially forbade homosexuality and even "particular friendships" among students. But everyone — staff and students — knew of countless affairs all the time. I discussed this issue a few years ago with Fr Michael Keane, the founder of the Knock Marriage Bureau who was a student in Maynooth in the 1940s. He did not seem to think that full sex had happened in Maynooth in his day, but he did say in his best Mayo accent: "You might hould a fella's hand but Jaysus it'd never go as far as a kish (kiss)!" I believe that some Maynooth students did have full sexual intercourse; in fact, several have told me of such happenings. But I imagine that in the 1940s these things were kept even quieter than they were in the 1970s.

When I entered Clonliffe in 1970 there were 120 seminarians there aged between eighteen and forty-five years old, though the vast majority were under thirty. Very many of them were handsome young men and of course all in their sexual prime. The authorities obviously realised that masturbation was a "serious problem". Regarding it as a "mortal sin" the Clonliffe authorities had the college spiritual director, Fr Tom O'Flynn, hold confessions early each morning before Mass. If you had masturbated during the night, you could not go to Holy Communion without confession. Otherwise you committed an even more grave sin, a sacrilege. If you did not get communion, the whole college would know you had masturbated the previous night! Many seminarians trooped into confession every morning by the dozen. They were called "the wankers" and Fr O'Flynn's early morning confessional was disrespectfully called "Wanker's Corner"! It was obvious from this situation that "bad thoughts" and "bad actions with yourself" were a major problem in Clonliffe — and indeed in every other seminary in the country and the world.

During the early 1970s, the President of Clonliffe, Bishop Joseph Carroll, called a senior student (now a Dublin priest) to his rooms to express concern over homosexuality in the college. Apparently there were a number of senior students, near ordination, having homosexual flings with younger students. A number of the students were encouraged to leave; though, for some inexplicable reason, a number of others were left alone, tolerated and ordained. It seemed that the nearer ordination you were the more your homosexual "failings" were tolerated. In the Clonliffe of my day, there were a small number of quite "predatory" homosexual senior students. After ordination, some went on to become quite predatory frequenters of the Dublin gay scene.

One junior student used to knock on my door in the early hours of the morning — on his way back from a senior student's bed — to weep about his love for the older student and the older student's apparent coldness to him. I was the one he came to for help to cope with the pressures of the relationship. The relationship was discovered by the Clonliffe authorities and the younger student was asked to leave while the older went on to ordination in spite of his homosexuality being known to the college authorities. After ordination, that older student became an active member of the Dublin gay scene and is, I imagine, active to this very day, one of the "prowlers" I referred to above.

Many Clonliffe students during my time there were members of Archbishop John Charles McQuaid's "Archbishop's Corps". This Corps was a uniformed guard of honour for the archbishop and all these young men had instant access to Dr McQuaid. Some of them were used by Dr McQuaid as "spies" around the diocese — checking out on priests' sermons, among other things. Quite a few of the homosexual affairs that I knew of at Clonliffe took place between former members of the Archbishop's Corps. I sensed and sense, rightly or wrongly, that there was a very strong gay undertone to this organisation.

As soon as the new seminarian entered Clonliffe, Archbishop McQuaid made sure that sex became a major preoccupation of theirs. Each of the 120 students was seen individually by Archbishop McQuaid for up to two or three hours. The seminarians would sit at the side of his desk in his darkened office with a great big fire blazing. The Archbishop would press his foot painfully upon theirs and tell them the "facts of life". He would make drawings of the penis, the testicles and the vagina. To demonstrate penetration, he would use one finger as a penis and his other fingers would form a vagina. Finally, he would give the seminarians a little crucifix to grasp during the night when they were tempted to masturbate. Anybody attending those interviews without a sexual hang-up would not leave it so free. It was bizarre.

Did I have sex in Clonliffe? I did not. I did get huge crushes on several fellow students and several got huge crushes on me. We were friends, went out together on harmless leisure occasions and maybe sat or lay close. But I did not have the confidence to take things further and neither did they. Even if we had had the confidence, the guilt and repression would have killed us afterwards. But of course, I was a regular customer at Father O'Flynn's early morning confessional.

IN JUNE 1973 I WAS EXPELLED from Clonliffe College for disobedience of the rules and skipping boring lectures. I was told that I showed a lack of seriousness about my vocation. I was devastated. But I soon got a place for the following September in St John's College, Waterford.

That summer I was to have my first adult sexual encounter. I was twenty-one and so was he.

During the previous year I had been to Scotland on a Legion of Mary expedition to convert people to Catholicism. During my time in Scotland, I met a young Catholic man my own age whose identity I want to protect by calling him Tom. Tom was tall and handsome and had a very winning Glasgow accent. I fell for Tom and he seemed to want to be close to me. We corresponded for some months and then we arranged for him to visit me at my Dublin home for a few days in July. We had a few lovely days of friendship and companionship together. We shared a room with twin beds. Everything inside me wanted to share one bed with him. On the last night he was staying, at two in the morning, our hands reached out to each other across the space between the beds. The feeling was electric. He joined me in my bed. I had never been so close to someone I was sexually attracted to. I thought I would faint. I could hardly breathe. We touched each other briefly and it was all over for me in, literally, twenty seconds of wet pleasure and confusion. We did not talk afterwards or sleep together. I was stunned — and immediately assailed by an enormous tidal wave of guilt. I had just committed the biggest "mortal sin" I had ever committed. I could not sleep.

At seven in the morning, I rang a priest's doorbell. A sleepy head came out the bedroom window. "Father, I need confession," I blurted out. "Have you committed a bloody murder?" enquired the tired and cynical priest. In my mind I had almost done worse. Inside, I confessed to him and literally wept on the floor. "Father, will this stop me being a priest?" I begged. "Only if you do it again," said the priest, obviously wishing he could return to his bed. I got my absolution and penance and caught the bus for the city centre.

I went to early morning Mass at the Blessed Sacrament Chapel in D'Olier Street. The priest came out to begin Mass. His first words were, "My dear people, you are welcome to Mass this morning. It is the twenty-second of July — the feast day of Mary Magdala — the great sinner who became a great saint." Something snapped inside me and I there and then fell in love with Mary Magdala. I later placed her image on my ordination memorial card. I have had a lifetime affair with her ever since.

What a first adult sexual encounter I had had! How I now wish I could have allowed myself to enjoy it! I never heard from Tom again. I think he was later expelled from a seminary for being gay. But to this day I keep his photograph and remember our early "fumblings" with affection, sadness and respect.

I WENT TO SAINT JOHN'S COLLEGE, Waterford in September 1973, and immediately preferred it to Clonliffe. It was a poorer college and the food and living conditions were more sparse than in Clonliffe. But it was a small friendly college, with just sixty students, and the staff were much more down-to-earth and student-friendly. Soon after my arrival I went to the dean to ask if I could bring a visiting nun friend to my room. He wondered why I even had to ask. In Clonliffe, women were not allowed past the ground floor.

I feel in general that there was less homosexuality in Waterford than there had been at Clonliffe. There were a lot of students there from rural areas and a lot of late vocation students. I knew of the odd homosexual incident involving students and indeed the odd heterosexual affair between students and young women. Yet somehow Waterford was a much less repressed place and sex was not such a big issue.

However, it was in Waterford that I truly fell in love for the first time. Soon after I went there I noticed that a slightly younger student was taking a great interest in me. He always seemed to be "hanging around" me. He always managed to sit at the same table as me for meals, and on many occasions I would find him standing alone and idle on the corridor where my room was. Initially I thought nothing of it, but eventually I became curious and later still interested and we formed a lovely friendship. Again, out of deference for his privacy, I will call him Gary.

Gary and I spent as much time as possible together. We would go into Waterford town together every day and on occasional trips to Dublin and further afield. As our friendship grew more intense, we would lie on a bed beside each other, embracing or holding hands — just drinking in each other's personality, presence and personal smell. We nearly always lay together in cassocks! Was that fear and protection? We would both have been conscious of our mutual sexual arousal.

One study period Gary came to my room. He was on the way back from a shower and wearing only a cassock. I could see the flesh of his side and legs through the pocket slits in the cassock. I was studying at my desk. He came over, sat right up on my knee facing me, put his nose about an inch from mine and said, "I've come to get you." I could feel the sexual desire and intensity pulsating from him. I was deeply aroused and wanted to respond to him but was stopped again by feelings of guilt and the fear of being banished from the priesthood. A lot of hugging seemed to get us over that "crisis" but I was frustrated because I could not "be myself" with Gary.

By this stage we knew we were madly in love with each other. This incident was often repeated but always with the same non-orgasmic outcome. Gary asked to sleep with me. I was afraid. We compromised: he would bring his mattress around and sleep on my floor and we would hold hands all night — that is, after we each masturbated ourselves separately from the sense of frustration. When

Gary and I were away together we slept in separate beds or sleeping bags but always held hands all night.

Eventually I did something that ended our relationship. I went to confession and talked to the confessor about my relationship with Gary. Gary was so hurt that I had discussed him, even in confession. He never forgave me. To this day I bitterly regret the hurt and distress I caused him.

In one sense Gary had an advantage over me. He had been sexually active since the age of twelve — with peers, with teachers and with priests. By the time he met me, he had lost all his inhibitions and repressions. He spent one holiday in Rome with a priest. He and the priest stayed in bed every day having sex except for when the priest had to go and say Mass. He would then return to Gary.

I loved Gary and I truly regret having hurt him, even though I myself was a total prisoner of repression, fear and guilt and would never have intended hurting him. I have not been in contact with him for many years. Because of my church notoriety and high profile he will, I imagine, often have been reminded of me. I sometimes wonder what he thinks of me now and how terribly I handled his love for me. I hope that by now he has understood and forgiven me.

DURING MY TIME IN WATERFORD I consulted the priest Professor Feicin O'Doherty of the Department of Psychology at University College Dublin about my homosexual orientation. His advice was strict and uncompromising — there must be no fantasising, there must be no masturbating. To combat these things I was to control my imagination by fasting and doing penance. His was the traditional advice. I cannot recall if it was him or others who advised the stone cold showers in the middle of the night as the sure cure for erections and "bad thoughts". But try as I might, the fastings and penances did not work, the fantasies and thoughts abounded and I never quite got around to trying the cold showers.

Sex in the Seminary

I LEFT THE SEMINARY IN 1976, nearly thirty years ago, and of course a lot has changed in the Church and in seminaries since. However, I have always maintained contact with seminarians. Quite a few seminarians, just like quite a few priests, come to see me or communicate with me covertly. If the hierarchy knew they saw me or were in touch with me, their "clerical careers" would be over. I call them my "Nicodemuses". Nicodemus was the man who, for fear of the Pharisees of his day, used to come to Jesus "under the cover of darkness". So I am kept right up to date on current happenings in dioceses, religious orders and seminaries. The hierarchy know this and, to put it mildly, are quite perturbed about it.

One young man, who trained in an Irish seminary, gave me a detailed account of his experiences, some of which I have included below:

> When I decided at the age of eighteen that I wanted to become a priest, I knew that I was gay. I didn't run into the church to hide behind the cloth or to deny myself, but instead of experiencing an atmosphere of acceptance and a time when I could deal with my sexuality in such a manner that would allow me to square my sexuality with the dogmas of my church, I very soon stumbled across a secluded environment where hypocrisy was rooted to the core.
>
> I entered seminary at a time when the sexuality of priests was very much under the gaze of public scrutiny, especially after high-profile paedophile court cases, homosexual and heterosexual scandals, which saw bishops and priests being uncovered for having hidden sexual relationships. To counter this, and to make sure that every seminarian was made aware of their sexual identity, the seminary ran a three-day workshop on sexuality in which they brought in two trained psychologists to assist us in exploring what it meant to be a sexual person. It was the worse three days possible, because from the start it was directed under the belief that every seminarian in the room was "straight", and for the vast majority of us who were gay, the issue of homosexuality was not discussed until after the two psychologists left and one of the deans came in to address the subject. What he said was short and to the point and it went something like this: "Lads, I'm only going to say two things to you. The showers are communal. When you're in there, under no circumstances are you to

feel up another lad, even if he wants you to feel him up. Secondly, under my watch there are to be no sexual acts of any kind between you. I warn you — one fuck and you're fucked! Right lads, time for supper." After hearing this, I knew this man was not one I could trust with the truth about my sexuality.

By the time my first week in the seminary was over I was to read in the papers that a priest had dropped dead of a heart attack in a Dublin gay sauna, and even more shockingly that there was another priest there to give him the Last Rites! By the end of the day, the deans were doing the coffee rounds trying to convince us that it wasn't a gay sauna but a gay bar! How futile, I thought.

I could see where this priest could have caught the flavour for this type of activity, because in the college there was an indoor swimming pool for the personal use of the students and the priests. Three things happened in there that made me never go back through the door again. The first time I was there I was getting dressed beside a priest member of the teaching staff and the whole time this priest kept eying my crotch and my rear. Secondly, when I returned from my swim that day my boxers were gone! Only three people had been in the building the whole time — the lifeguard, who stayed beside the pool all the time, the priest and myself. Thirdly, one day during my first fortnight in the seminary, I was invited by a group of lads to play "water polo". Quite quickly I realised that it wasn't water polo they had in mind but man to man physical contact under the water that was sexually arousing many of them.

Within a short space of time I had come to see the sub-gay culture that existed within the seminary. I didn't have to look too far because it was there, and had I decided to physically express my sexuality I would have had plenty of opportunity to do so. The vast grounds and woodlands surrounding the seminary was rife with gay cruisers and gay seminarians went cruising there at night time. At all times of the day and night, men were seen around the place, hiding behind trees or standing near the goal posts waiting for their eyes to meet with another guy. Seminarians themselves were known to have sex in each other's rooms, and in the early hours of the morning they would cruise the senior corridor, commonly known as the "Pink Corridor", and upon entering the toilets they could have hand and oral relief from fellow seminarians.

For a period of several weeks during Saturday evening adoration devotions, a very camp student would place himself opposite me and

Sex in the Seminary

for an hour and a half would stare me out. Spotting this, a deacon from my home diocese came to warn me not to entertain him in any way, because this student, who was very "in" with the current president, was so screwed up that he took delight in "outing" other students. I couldn't believe it. In the church, he was sitting there looking for me to make a move just so he could go running to the president and "out" me for making a pass at him!

Over the years, many seminarians left, some of their own accord, while others were often ordered out, sometimes with absolutely no reason given to them by the seminary authorities.

During the whole of my training, there is one incident that remains clearest of all in my mind. A new student arrived and he was extremely attractive. Right away everyone wanted to get to know him and he became very popular. Within a few weeks it was clear to see that he was loving the attention he was getting from the lads and he would tease some of them over the dinner table with rude jokes and sexual innuendo. He was very fond of buying gifts for other students. After a conversation one day he recognised from the smell of my aftershave that I liked a certain brand and in my room he spotted a whiskey I liked. The following day he knocked at my room door and I opened it to find him standing there with my favourite aftershave in one hand and my favourite whiskey in the other. There was no doubt about it but that he was a very generous guy, but we were all wondering how an eighteen-year-old seminarian could afford to keep buying all these expensive gifts. It didn't take us long to find out.

The young seminarian was the sexual partner of an older priest and several times a week the priest would arrive at the seminary and he and the seminarian would be locked into the seminarian's rooms for three or four hours. It was quite clear to us that the two of them were not playing tiddlywinks! The two of them were very close and would regularly head off on highly expensive holidays and weekend breaks. They once stayed in a top hotel in London and the seminarian showed me some glow-in-the-dark condoms that had been left by their expensive hotel bedside. It was an open secret that they were having a sexual relationship and they were taking little or no steps to hide it. For years it went either unnoticed or not acted upon by the seminary authorities and the priest and members of the college staff were friends. But it came to a head when there was a danger of the story getting into the national press and the seminarian was removed from the college.

The saddest thing for me over the years has been watching the number of good students leave the seminary simply because they didn't "fit in". The problem was that amid the sub-culture of homosexuality that ran strongly through the seminary, they obviously didn't feel right, and instead of recognising this they were convinced in their own hearts that they didn't have a calling to a priestly vocation. I have seen others leave and being dumped from the seminary, broken men, many of whom have yet to move on with their lives. I have seen a few good guys make it through, while I have also seen the church ordain the most repressed and psychologically mixed-up people that I have come across. Yet, saddest of all for me as a gay man is this — our Catholic Church today is run by predominantly gay clergy, very few of whom are free to live their priestly vocation to the fullest, and instead of a clergy free in spirit, our seminaries are fostering priests with no individuality and I fear for what their future and the future of our church holds.

I WAS IN SEMINARY FROM 1970 until 1976 and of course during that time my relationship with God, my spirituality, evolved and developed. In the seminary I had access to daily Mass, daily meditation and prayer, spiritual direction and the celebration of the Divine Office — what we now call the breviary or the daily prayer of the church. It used to involve coming to prayer seven times a day. Since Vatican II, it is five times — Office of Readings, Morning Prayer, Midday Prayer, Evening Prayer and Night Prayer. I enjoyed all of these spiritual exercises and they certainly helped me develop a deeper spirituality.

We also had several retreats each year which I enjoyed and which brought me closer to God. The longest retreat I undertook was at the beginning of my second year in Clonliffe. I engaged in the famous Jesuit thirty-day retreat — thirty days of silence, prayer, meditation, self-examination, confession and devotions. It was a highly intensive retreat and a few of my classmates had to fall out as the intensity was getting to them emotionally and mentally. I survived it because I have always loved retreats and because of my sense of humour. Even in the midst of this solemn retreat I was making people laugh daily by imitating the retreat master's voice and his walk to church in his squeaky sandals. Very often I had everyone in the small Clonliffe oratory in fits of laughter. I've always believed that laughter is an emotional and mental life-saver.

I had my own very meaningful devotions too: my visits to the chapel by day and by night for a quiet prayer, to light a candle or to pray the Stations of the Cross, the fourteen meditations on Christ's last journey from Jerusalem to Calvary where He died.

I also loved reading spiritual biographies and books. I learned about all the saints and the various messages of their lives and came to own and treasure several Lives of the Saints. I also had a very early interest in those early saints we call the Desert Fathers. I was a very idealistic and spiritual young man looking for spiritual heroes, and the history of the church abounded with them — St John Bosco, St John Vianney, St Thérèse, St Teresa of Avila, St John of the Cross, St Paul of the Cross, St Francis of Assisi, St Dominic . . . the list of heroes was endless and I revelled in the biographies of them all.

Then and now, I have been greatly helped towards human and spiritual maturity and growth by many authors. I fell in love with the writings of Dom Columba Marmion's. Marmion had been a student at Clonliffe, a priest of the Dublin diocese and eventually a very famous Benedictine monk and abbot. I also greatly admired and began to take an interest in Brother Charles de Foucauld (1858–1916) who led an early life of debauchery and later became a Cistercian monk, a priest, a pastor and a simple spiritual master, in the middle of the Sahara Desert. De Foucauld's simple theology of life — love of God in the Eucharist and love of God in the brother — appealed to me. It pleases me greatly that Brother de Foucauld's long overdue canonisation is now finally being advanced. Other great writers who have been my spiritual companions over the years include Archbishop Helder Camara of Brazil; Archbishop Oscar Romero of El Salvador; Leonardo Boff, the South American Franciscan theologian silenced by Rome; Fr Matthew Fox, the Dominican; Fr Henri Nouwen, the Dutch spiritual writer whose closeted homosexuality was a lifelong burden; Hans Küng, the brilliant Jesuit theologian who has been hounded and persecuted by the Vatican; Fr George Tyrrell, the convert to Catholicism and later Jesuit writer and prophet, who was persecuted in life and death by the Catholic Hierarchy in England; Dietrich Bonhoeffer, the German pastor who suffered under the Nazis and who wrote so meaningfully about Christian discipleship; Thomas Merton, the Trappist monk and spiritual great; and of course Cardinal John Henry Newman, the convert to Catholicism who has given me the words I have already had inscribed on my headstone: "Conscience is the aboriginal vicar of Christ."

When the way was dark and when there was no one around to turn to, these and other authors have kept me company, inspired me to keep going and filled my heart and head with wisdom, vision and hope.

I AM ALWAYS VERY SADDENED when I hear priests say things like: "I haven't opened a book since the day I left college." I am firmly convinced that a major part of the Church's problems at the moment is connected to the fact that far too many priests don't pray and don't feed a prayer life with spiritual reading. The Jewish holy man Ibn Tibbon said it all: "Make books your companions; let your bookshelves be your gardens; bask in their beauty, gather their fruit, pluck their roses, take their spices and myrrh. And when your soul be weary, change from garden to garden, and from prospect to prospect." There can be no spirituality, no spiritual life and no wisdom without spiritual reading.

When I was in the seminary, there were two principal aspects to seminary life: the intellectual, which received the most attention, and the spiritual. I was most taken and most interested in the spiritual. I had no ambitions to become an academic or a teacher. I wanted to be an ordinary, good parish priest and always work "on the ground" with the people. While the seminary put us through our paces in terms of celebrating Mass and religious exercises there was no real emphasis at all on developing us as mature spiritual people. We were not properly spiritually formed. And, of course, there was no attention at all to the integration of spirituality with sexuality or even with "real life".

The seminary failed us all most miserably when it came to helping us develop a proper spirituality that would see us through all the ups and downs of life. It gave us what it gave the laity — religion and dogma and devotion — but no spirituality that could be our rock. Many priests left seminary with religion and religious knowledge but not a deep personal faith. They left the seminary knowing a lot about Jesus Christ but not knowing Jesus Christ. They also left the seminary hugely sexually repressed and dysfunctional. Was it any wonder that many a priest coped by hitting the booze, becoming addicted gamblers or materialists or engaging in every kind of secret sexual activity?

I left the seminary in 1976 with a deep personal faith — thanks to God alone, and not to the seminary or myself — a faith that has lasted me through thick and thin for nearly thirty years now. But I received that faith and have maintained it, not because of the institution and my training, but in spite of it.

The greatest crisis in the Catholic Church today is not the sex scandals or the other corruptions but rather the fact that bishops and priests have little or no true spiritual faith and little or no prayer life!

A SPIRITUAL LIFE HAS TO BE WORKED AT and comes, in great part, through greater knowledge of oneself. For me, counselling contributed greatly to my spiritual growth. I have already described some of the wonderful people who have helped me along this path. The most serious and useful counselling I received was with therapist Jarlath Benson in Belfast. Jarlath is a practitioner of psychosynthesis, a therapy that it is very holistic and takes account of the spiritual as well as the psychological. Over several years I faced all my demons with Jarlath. I have the highest admiration for him. He knew when to be silent — which was most of the time. He knew when to challenge — which was needed. But he also knew when to drop that very occasional little word of understanding and encouragement. A separate book would be required to deal with all these years of counselling and the many complicated issues that arose. But it was a great journey and voyage from emotional and psychological captivity to freedom. At the same time I was reviewing my faith and my spirituality and was travelling the journey from fear and guilt to the freedom of a son of God.

Over the years, I have talked to some other people as well — psychiatrists, therapists, clergymen — from each of whom I received something, other building blocks for my little temple of freedom. One clergyman/therapist I spoke to asked me to spontaneously draw a picture of how I felt. Without any great planning, I drew the picture of a great big smouldering volcano. On top of the volcano there was a massive rock stopping it erupting. There was so much going on below the surface — fear, anxiety, guilt, anger, hurt, sexual and sensual desire — and this great big rock of denial of my real self and having to cope was just about keeping the eruption at bay. But what a price I was paying!

The eruption occurred in 1987, and it manifested itself psychosomatically. I developed Crohn's disease. Crohn's is a serious ulceration of the bowel. It causes bleeding, pain, weight loss and occasionally even death. The doctors in Belfast tried to control the disease with conventional treatments such as steroids. Steroids are a great drug but how awful and unnatural they make you feel! Eventually they failed to control it and I was admitted to the Royal Victoria Hospital in Belfast where I had major surgery — a bowel resection. They removed three parts of my bowel. I felt very, very sick. But once again I was blessed to meet a most wonderful surgeon, Mr Roy Maxwell. He was at my bed three or four times a day or during the night when I needed him. He is a most modest man and will be appalled by my praise.

Soon afterwards, I heard of Professor John Hermon Taylor of St George's Hospital in Tooting, South London. He was treating Crohn's in a controversial way, blasting the body with TB-type drugs. Against medical advice in Belfast, I took myself to the professor — a controversial professor for a controversial priest! He put me on a cocktail of drugs. For three weeks I thought I was going to die. Then my body got used to them and I have never looked back. At a check-up in December 2000 doctors could find no trace of my Crohn's! With the help of the professor (and God) I seem to be in a very stable remission. As I write, Professor Taylor is just months away from introducing a vaccine for Crohn's disease.

But there was another vital aspect to my Crohn's "recovery". I knew that it was stress-related. I got it a year after Bishop Cahal Daly dumped me from the diocese and I had had an ongoing battle with him. I used my years of counselling and therapy to deal with my stress levels and the management of my life. I also used aromatherapy and massage.

There was a time when I would fight any fight. Nowadays I fight the important fights and let the unimportant ones go. Maybe I'm getting wise. Years ago someone said to me: "Buckley, I've never doubted your courage. Sometimes I doubt your wisdom." Maybe these days I have a little of both?

Everybody has baggage. Everybody needs counselling. Not everybody needs formal counselling. Many people get it informally from a lover, a partner, a friend. But if you bottle things up, eventually they will blow or you will get a serious physical illness. That which is pushed from the mind will attack the body. I remember a doctor saying to me in the late 1980s, "Pat, if you had been capable of having a good mental breakdown you would never have got Crohn's disease."

I worry about people who bottle things up and don't talk about what's going wrong inside them. Men are worse than women in this sense. Perhaps that at least partly explains why we in Ireland have one of the highest rates of young male suicide in the world? Talking and crying are nature's way of giving us release.

MY ORDINATION DAY, 6 JUNE 1976, the Feast of Pentecost, was one of the happiest days of my life. By that time, I had longed to be a priest for twenty-one years. Finally, I had reached the summit of a passionately desired mountain. Quite simply, on that day and on the days that followed, I was deliriously happy. I felt good about God, good about myself, good about life and looked forward to a wonderful priestly future.

During the ordination ceremony in Waterford Cathedral, I felt I was in the anteroom of Heaven itself. As I lay prostrated on the floor awaiting the bishop's hands upon my head, I felt the intense presence of God. But words are inadequate to describe my ordination day. I think I must have felt like Peter and John on that day when Jesus took them up the mountain and was transfigured before their eyes and they saw His glory as God. On my ordination day, I could easily have used Peter's mountain-top words: "Lord, it is very good for us to be here."

Looking back now, and thinking particularly of my sexuality, at the time of my ordination I was in total denial. On that day, I really felt that God and the grace I was experiencing made everything else pale into insignificance.

I haven't lost my passion for priesthood. Quite the contrary. But I have lost my 1976 starry-eyed naïveté. I now understand, after a thirty-year spiritual and sexual journey, that religious euphoria is not a permanent and total antidote to the sexual propensity and appetite.

In 1976, I was a spiritual and sexual scizophrenic. I hope that now, in 2005, I am more integrated and that my sexuality and spirituality live happily together in an older and wiser soul. Over the next few chapters, I would like to describe some of the milestones in that journey.

Chapter Five

DESIRE AND DENIAL

Teacher: "What are the sins of omission, my child?"
Child: "They're the sins we ought to commit and don't!"
— *Anonymous*

I HAVE ALWAYS REGARDED MYSELF as singularly unattractive and in fact have often, throughout my life, felt painfully undesirable. Very often sexual abuse victims see themselves as "ugly" and "dirty" anyway. But also as a child and teenager I was overweight and took an awful lot of flak in school, enduring a lot of name-calling. It has left me with quite a complex which survives to this present day although it is not at all as bad now and I cope well with it. I am still conscious of my weight but of course these days I realise that it is simply a lifestyle issue. Like many more in our modern world I need to be more careful about my eating and exercising habits.

In spite of this, even I — a self-accusing "ugly duckling" — have had my suitors! Some were welcome and some were not.

I HAD KNOWN THE ABBOT since my student days and used to talk to him as an advisor and confessor. He always sat too close to me for comfort — knees touching, feet touching and his hand on my hand or knee. He brought every conversation quickly around to sex. He was in his seventies in 1976 and he told me that during his forty-plus years in the monastery he had had eighteen sexual partners — mainly men but the occasional woman. He liked to talk about his sexual partners and what they did. He also liked to talk a lot about genitalia and about his own body — his masturbation habit and various bits of surgery he had had. I always found his conversation very discomforting and embarrassing. I certainly found the thoughts of having a sexual encounter with him very repulsive. But I did feel very sorry for him as he seemed to have lived a life of great sexual frustration and guilt.

He never directly misbehaved with me but he sat so close and was so suggestive it was quite an ordeal. He made his intentions perfectly clear. But I think in my own compassionate way I made my intentions clear to him also. There was always a great tension in our friendship. He is dead now and I am sure that he is happy in Heaven. He did a lot of good in his lifetime and I believe that God is great at forgetting our human weaknesses and rewarding our efforts to be good.

EARLY IN MY PRIESTHOOD, on two separate occasions, I was propositioned by two canons. I was ministering at the time in Wales and was returning to Ireland for a holiday. An old canon of my acquaintance asked if he could travel with me. I saw no problem and agreed. I drove and we got the ferry from Wales to Wexford and I then drove him to Cork where I was to drop him off to visit his family. We had to spend one night in Cork City together and we booked into a room with twin beds in a small hotel.. A nice young chambermaid showed us our room. As soon as she left, the octogenarian canon, without any warning, pushed me back on one of the beds, jumped on top of me and began to kiss and grope me. Just then, the door opened again and the chambermaid reappeared with our key, saw the two clerics on the bed, gave a squeak and ran out. I quickly extricated myself from under the canon and told him it wasn't on. He was deeply offended and tried to persist. I left the room, went for a long walk, had a bit of dinner and didn't return to the room until one in the morning. I went to my own bed and went asleep. Next morning when I woke up, the canon was gone. I went on to Dublin for my family holiday.

On later occasions, when I met the canon at social events, he always gave me a look of contempt and ignored me. He seemed convinced that I, not he, had done something wrong! The poor old man had a very big sexual frustration problem. A couple of years later, I learned with sadness that he had to be taken out of his presbytery in the middle of the night screaming hysterically about his sexuality and frustrations. He had told me early on in our brief friendship that I could make progress in my church career if I did sexual favours for my superiors; he told me that he knew of priests who became bishops in that way.

ON ANOTHER OCCASION, not long after this, I wanted to borrow a minibus from another parish priest, a man in his late forties. I telephoned him and he invited me to call to make arrangements. I was sitting in his sitting-room and we were having a cup of tea. He stood up and walked over to my armchair and sat on the arm. I felt very crowded but did not suspect initially that there was any sexual intention. Then, without warning, he leaned down, began to kiss me on the lips and used a force which pinned my head to the back of the chair. A cup of tea was spilt and a slight struggle ensued before I got free. I said to him, "What did you do that for?" He blushed, left the room, came back with the bus keys and I left. Again, whenever we met subsequently on social and church occasions, he was very cool with me.

Both men handled these situations very badly. To my mind, there is nothing wrong with any two consenting adults having sex in private. But I cannot understand anybody making a sexual move on someone without first of all checking to see if the advance is welcomed. I have never been angry with these men. I just think that their level of sexual frustration must have been very high. I also blame the Catholic Church for enforcing obligatory celibacy on all priests. It does not work. It drives some priests to alcohol and drugs. It drives others to frustration and mental illness. It drives many priests into having secret heterosexual and homosexual relationships.

ONE OF THE LONELIEST PERIODS of my life was my time in Wales as a young priest in 1976 and 1977. I was homesick for Ireland and my family. I was missing the companionship of my six years in the seminary. The parish priest, Fr Driscoll, was to my mind nothing short of a sadist. He mentally tortured me in every way he could. I had to be in bed at nine at night. I was not allowed visitors or telephone calls. I was not allowed to make myself a cup of tea in the kitchen. He used to say to me, "Irishmen's brains are hanging between their legs." I was chaplain to the local hospital but he would not allow me to visit the maternity ward. According to the parish priest, "Irishmen have a fetish about pregnant women and swollen bellies. You'll not indulge that fantasy in my parish." From what I heard, many curates before me had had to go through similar torture. I became unhappy and depressed. I talked to the Archbishop, who told me the parish priest was "a very holy man. Offer it up and it will make you holy too." I could not. I became more and more depressed and eventually started having panic attacks. One day it came to a head and I broke down and sobbed while stopped at traffic lights.

Right in the middle of this period, an uncle rang me to tell me that my cousin was in trouble with the police in Ireland; he had been dabbling on the edges of the drug scene. My uncle begged me to take him to Wales. I was living with a housekeeper and a parish priest who didn't want one Buckley in their house, never mind two! Nevertheless I agreed and my cousin came to me in Wales. For three weeks I prayed solidly and begged God to help me find my cousin a place to live and a job. Nothing happened and I was under huge pressure within the presbytery to move him on.

One morning after Mass when the church was empty I went in and stood in front of the altar and said: "Fuck you, God. I am over here in Wales and have left my family and my country and everything to work for you. My cousin is here and I need a job and a place for him to live and I have prayed and prayed and have gotten nowhere. Do you not care about us and the pressure I'm under? Fuck you anyway!"

I stormed out of the church and was having my breakfast when the telephone rang. It was a local hotel and they were offering my cousin an interview for a job as a part-time barman. I drove him to the interview. He was two hours in the hotel. He came out and sat into the car and I asked: "Did you get the job?" "No," he replied. I was devastated. "But they offered me a different job," he said. "They offered me trainee manager — and there's a live-in flat with the job!" I was flabbergasted. Our two problems had been solved in one fell swoop.

I went straight back to the church and stood in front of the altar and addressed myself again to "Big G". I said to Him, "First of all, I just want to thank you for what you've done. Secondly, I want to apologise for swearing at you earlier. But thirdly, if it takes a bit of swearing and a row to get you moving you can expect a bit more of it from me from now on!"

I was very grateful to God for what had happened and I did give Him the credit. But there are times in life — times of pressure, suffering and loneliness, when we become totally exasperated, even with God. That's the time for straight-talking. God must get awfully tired of all the millions and millions of "Our Fathers" that people fling at Him everyday. I think it must be very refreshing for Him when someone calls out to him from the depth of their pain or sufferings — even if they do use a bit of building-site language!

When I approached the auxiliary bishop about my problem with the parish priest, he suggested that there was something wrong with me mentally and he asked me to visit a psychiatrist. I readily agreed. I had nothing to fear. I spent an afternoon with the psychiatrist in his home. He gave me a letter saying that there was nothing wrong with me — except that I was living in a presbytery hell. The Archbishop rejected the psychiatrist's findings and insisted I stay in the parish. He told me if I left he would designate me a *"fugitivus"*, a fugitive in church law, and see to it that I never worked again as a priest! I told him I would prefer to be a fugitivus than a patient in a psychiatric hospital. I left for Ireland. He kept his word and declared me a Canon Law criminal — a priest without permission to minister. I was a fairly broken man, but not totally broken and not then, or ever, a quitter.

I SPENT NINE HARD MONTHS AT HOME in Dublin, drawing the dole and working as a volunteer in the Legion of Mary Morning Star Hostel for homeless men by the Richmond Hospital in Dublin. During these months I also celebrated Mass for the homeless men and for the homeless women and prostitutes who lived next door at the Regina Coeli Hostel. I found my hostel work, whether it was making beds, serving food, washing dishes or celebrating Mass, very meaningful. I was a priest, after all, following humbly in the footsteps of Christ, and what kind of work could have been more Christ-like?

After Wales and Dublin I arrived in Belfast in the summer of 1978 to take up an appointment at St Peter's Cathedral, attached to the Divis Flats in the Falls Road. As I made a new start I was very insecure. The insecurity showed itself again with a tendency to have panic attacks, sometimes in awkward places like the confessional and when saying Mass. I did consult a very kind Belfast psychiatrist and he was very understanding and helpful. He prescribed some valium to tide me over the most difficult times and eventually the crisis subsided. At this time I think that my loneliness and sexual conflict were working away at a deeper and only semi-conscious level. It is hard to ignore and be out of touch with such basic powers and instincts and for there not to be profound emotional and mental repercussions.

During difficult days in Divis Flats in Belfast when I was getting on so well with the people but so badly with the clergy in the presbytery, I also came under great mental pressure. One night I was even physically attacked by the parish priest Fr Vincent McKinley. I talked to my GP, Dr Joe Hendron (the SDLP politician) and he was sympathetic and gave me some more valium. I also chose to talk to the consultant psychiatrist Peter Curran at Belfast's Mater Hospital briefly. He was as helpful as he could be. I did discuss my sexuality with him. He gave me some valium too!

Eventually, through my late twenties and right through my thirties the sexual conflict became more and more of a struggle — a struggle that had to be faced. I knew eventually that I had to engage in some serious therapy and counselling to sort it all out and to come to a resolution. I could never have talked to my Bishop, Cahal Daly. I found him totally unapproachable, lacking in compassion and as they say, "so heavenly as to be no earthly use"!

FOR A NUMBER OF YEARS I had a very difficult friendship with a religious brother. We had met at a bus stop in Dublin when I was a seminarian in Clonliffe and we began a conversation. I was twenty at the time and he was in his fifties. When my bus came he handed me his card and invited me to call at his monastery for tea sometime. I did ring him and went for tea one afternoon.

From the very beginning of our friendship I sensed a huge loneliness in the man and when I was with him there was an amazing tension between us that I can now call a sexual tension. He was obviously a very repressed homosexual and he filled his life with boys and young men. He worked in an institution that looked after boys between the ages of ten and eighteen and he spent all his waking hours with these boys. He also hung around the swimming pool where the boys undressed, dressed and swam. I was to learn later, through past students, that he had had sexual encounters with some of the boys.

This brother brought me on several pilgrimages to Lourdes and on a couple of trips in Ireland. He always insisted we share a hotel room and I always dreaded the experience. He would sit on his bed enveloped in a palpable psychosexual trauma watching me getting very carefully and modestly dressed and undressed. He would stare uncontrollably at my genitalia and buttocks through my underwear. The situation was so tense and so sad. In one way my heart went out to him. In another way I was always slightly afraid of him. The sexual tension eventually led to a deterioration in our friendship and we saw little of each other. For the last few years of his life he sank into a black, black depression and I'm sure death came to him as a release and a friend. He was a living embodiment of what a life of sexual repression and guilt can do to a man. When I think back on him now, I feel very sad but I am glad that he is no longer trapped in his hell.

I HAVE ALWAYS FOUND IT VERY EASY to relate to women and be very free with them. This comes, I think, from growing up with six sisters. Girls and women have always been just a normal part of my life. I have worked with priests who had no sisters and was amazed at how women used to either enthral or throw them.

Over the years a number of women — including a few nuns — have attached themselves to me emotionally. Such situations are not always the easiest to handle. Within weeks of being ordained I was invited to a woman parishioner's bed! I was saying Mass one Sunday and this very attractive woman in her thirties was sitting in the front pew. She was tall and had a beautiful figure. She was dark-haired and dressed elegantly. During Mass I thought that she was smiling at me a lot. She was certainly staring through me. At communion time, I thought she deliberately allowed her lips to touch my fingers when I gave her communion, and after communion she actually winked at me.

After Mass I was standing outside the church greeting people as they left. She was last to leave. She took my hand and thanked me for a lovely Mass and sermon. She then said, with a very provocative look, "Would you like to call around to my house some night for your tea?" I said, in all innocence, "Yes, that would be fine." She then said, "We might even get around to having more than tea. Your predecessor was a regular visitor of mine. . . ." She left me in no doubt about what she meant and what was on offer. I never made it for the tea!

I'VE ALWAYS HAD A VERY GOOD RELATIONSHIP with nuns and I admire many of them greatly. On several occasions I was chaplain to convents — the St Louis Convent in Kilkeel, County Down, and the Cross and Passion Convent in Larne in County Antrim. I enjoyed saying Mass with and for the nuns. In general, I find that nuns are far more spiritual people than priests.

But in my priestly life I have had to face two very difficult situations when nuns became emotionally attached to, and maybe obsessed with, me. We used to meet regularly and go on little trips and out for the occasional meal. I allowed them to do various little domestic tasks for me. I made the big mistake of letting one of them do my personal washing and ironing!

In both cases the nuns, who were obviously very lonely, became quite overpowering and obsessive about me and it all ended in tears. Of course, I was never able to tell them that I was gay and that there was no hope of any future sexual or emotional relationship. Indeed, at the time I was very much in my own state of denial and repression and that would have raised problems too.

I DON'T WANT TO GIVE THE IMPRESSION that sexual desire was all one-way. Of course it wasn't. I have fallen in love or had "crushes" many times. In the early part of my life and priesthood this was a problem because I regarded all things sexual as sinful. Guilt and fear held me back greatly. But there were some little exceptions.

"Tommy" was from Belfast. When I met him I was twenty-six and he was nineteen. He had a good job and a very attractive girlfriend. Tommy used to attend my Mass occasionally. We got to know each other and he occasionally invited me to go out for a drink with him and his girlfriend. I enjoyed those nights out. I liked Tommy and indeed found him attractive but regarded him as "straight". Besides, I was still hung up and guilt-ridden and therefore not in the business of looking for or having sexual partners or contacts.

One night I was out with Tommy and his girlfriend. When his girlfriend went into the toilet, Tommy reached over, put his mouth to my ear and said, "Buckley, I fucking love you." I nearly choked on my beer. I looked at him and there were tears and pain in his eyes. Something snapped inside me and I felt deeply for him and really appreciative of his honesty. That night we went our separate ways. But on occasions afterwards when I would arrive home at night — even as late as two in the morning — Tommy would be standing at the corner waiting for me. He would linger and talk for ages. Eventually I would bring him in for tea or coffee. He would then be very silent and look so sad. I would ask him, "What's wrong?" He would say, "You know what's wrong." And I did.

One night we ended up talking in my sitting room. As it got later, he lay there silent on an armchair, his eyes closed. He looked so lonely and appealing. I knew he wanted me. And I wanted him.

I took him by the hand and led him to the bedroom. We lay on my bed. I caressed his hair and the bristles of his well-shaved beard. I loved his touch and his pleasant, manly smell. I was so totally inexperienced, though, that I was more or less paralysed. Eventually Tommy took the initiative. We had a brief sexual encounter — brief because of my nervousness — and we both achieved a hurried and only partially satisfactory orgasm. It was then time for him to go. I walked him home. I didn't want him to feel any guilt about our encounter. I gave him a hug and a goodnight kiss and told him I would call him the next day. I went back to bed.

Again the old guilt set in. I did not sleep well. I rose early and found a priest to hear my confession. Later I called on Tommy and asked him to come for a chat and a drive. He was embarrassed. We didn't go. In fact, we never really talked things through. Looking back, I once again regret how badly I handled such a beautiful and human occasion.

I know that Tommy is gay. I know that he lives abroad. I know that he is fonder of drugs and alcohol than is good for him. Tommy is more often in my thoughts and prayers than I'm sure he realises.

ON A NUMBER OF OCCASIONS in my life young teenage boys, including altar boys, got "crushes" on me and I found myself conscious of having to handle these situations very carefully. Many perfectly "normal" heterosexual boys go through a brief stage when they get "homosexual" crushes on another male, such as a teacher, a priest or a football coach. These are times of intense emotions for the teenager and the last thing they must be made to feel is rejected. Yet giving them the love and understanding they need and at the same time keeping clear boundaries can be difficult. But it can and has to be done.

Two people in particular come to mind. There was "John". He had emotionally very cold parents and got no affection. He became powerfully attached to me — so attached that he would weep about it. In 1978 he made me a beautiful little bookmark which I have to this day; it is a drawing of a big dog (me) sheltering a smaller dog (him) from the rain. On it is written: "From a faithful friend to a faithful friend." He and I went on trips together. I took him playing squash. I gave him my time. I deliberately visited his home and parents with him in case they were concerned. Eventually, John's crush went away. A number of years later he called to see me. He was anxious that I would meet his girlfriend. It was his way of saying to me, "In case you remember what I was like at fourteen, here is my girlfriend — I'm straight." I smiled and I got the message. I never doubted his sexuality in the first place. As they say in Belfast, I realised he was going through a "phrase"!

Then there was "Peter". I inherited Peter from a priest predecessor. He was a very intelligent young fellow with very strong views and an early and strong consciousness of his own homosexuality. His father was dead and he had a turbulent relationship with his mother. He spent a lot of time with me. I liked him a lot and enjoyed his company. I marvelled at his intensity and energy. He was very interested in the Church and wanted to become a priest. He was eventually ordained. He needed an awful lot of affection. I gave him affection and always observed boundaries. That was not easy. He literally was a whirlwind. But I was very touched when he came to see me recently and said, "Pat, I was some handful. I really appreciate the sensitive and caring way you handled me."

WHAT I LEARNED FROM THESE EXPERIENCES was that I was not totally ugly and undesirable, and that was an important human and spiritual lesson to learn. I used to have a poster of a monkey on my wall and underneath it read, *Lord, make me beautiful within*. I always felt I had inner beauty and I know that inner beauty is more lasting and important than outer beauty. But we all live in bodies in this world and most of find it important that some people, even one person, might regard us as "beautiful".

Very recently, I had a meeting one evening with a special new friend who told me that I was beautiful. I asked them what they meant. They told me they saw something very special in me, in my face, a light, that they found very beautiful. Of course, I believed them; their face said it all.

I have never been comfortable with thinking about myself in terms of the beautiful. But of course I should be able to think like this, especially as a Christian. We believe that we are made in the image and likeness of God and that our bodies are "temples of the Holy Spirit". So all our bodies are the image and likeness of God and the temples of the Holy Spirit must be truly beautiful. In that context, there is no one who is not beautiful.

The problem today is that the media is constantly bombarding us with what it regards as beautiful — the slim, tall, suntanned body with blue eyes and blonde hair. Many of us fall for that "image" and buy into it. A twenty-year-old man might be tall, slim, tanned, blue-eyed and blonde-haired; ten years later, he could be bald and fat. External beauty can fade fast; it is the internal beauty that is lasting and important.

When I celebrate marriages I can see that, when it comes to a life partner, people want more than external beauty. They really want the inner beauty. I like to think that there is someone out there for everyone. I think it must be very sad to live through a whole life and never be desired and thought beautiful by anyone. I am most grateful to God, to life and to people that there have been some along my way who found me desirable and beautiful. That feeling is not only good for the ego. It is also good for the soul. I think if we have experienced being desired by another human being it becomes easier for us to imagine and believe that God desires us, loves us and cares deeply for us.

Chapter Six

FALLING IN LOVE

"Let us not speak, for the love we bear one another —
Let us hold hands and look"
She, such a very ordinary little woman;
He, such a thumping crook;
But both, for a moment, little lower than the angels
In the teashop's ingle-nook
— Sir John Betjeman, "In a Bath Teashop"

I HAVE FULLY AND PUBLICLY acknowledged the fact that I am gay but as this book is an attempt at telling "the truth, the whole truth and nothing but the truth", I must also say that at times in my life I have fallen in love with men who were both heterosexual and homosexual. In fact, if I am asked, "What kind of man are you attracted to?" I would have to answer that I am most attracted to men who are masculine and "straight-acting". If I were attracted to women I would go for a woman and not an effeminate man. But it is to men that I am attracted. I have nothing against effeminate men, at all, whether they be straight or gay. But I find masculine (not macho) men most attractive.

At a non-sexual level — in my pastoral and caring work — I consider myself to be very good with men. I love to encourage men to acknowledge, explore and express their emotions and feelings. I believe that each of us, men and women, need to be in touch with both the feminine and masculine that is inside each of us. Men, real men, are able to cry as well as laugh. I love to see a husband being loving and expressive with his wife. I love to see a Dad being affectionate and demonstrative with his children. Many of the people I meet in my ministry are unhappy because their parents did not give them enough hugs and kisses or sit them on their knees for long enough when they were children. Love and affection are very under-used healers.

In the past twenty-five years I have become very close, emotionally, to a number of straight men. I will recount two stories:

WHEN I MET "MATTHEW" I was twenty-six and he was eighteen. He was the son of a cold and nervously unwell father and a very loving but ineffective mother. He was one of the most handsome young men I have ever met. He was very heterosexual and had his pick of the beautiful women who flocked around him at the pubs and clubs. He was also, according to himself, a very competent sexual partner with women.

But Matthew was desperately unhappy and he didn't know why. He had a huge darkness in his life and in his mind and he was nervous in the extreme. He would suffer from panic attacks at work. He came to me one day after work, in desperation, for help.

From the first moment I met Matthew I liked him. I felt deeply for his mental anguish and promised him I would do all I could to help him sort it out. We talked a lot, for hours and hours. Later, I brought him on trips to Dublin. We went to Lourdes together. I spent hours helping him to control his breathing to lessen his panic attacks. We also did some very basic therapy. But there seemed to be no way for Matthew to reach his dark core and explain it. It interfered with his work. He was hospitalised on a number of occasions. Nothing was working.

I remember one night going to see him in the psychiatric ward. He was like a "zombie" from his distress and medication. He recognised me but that was all. He could not speak. I got him to sit in a chair and I put my two hands on his head and I prayed for him like I had never prayed for anybody before. I even asked God to take his mental illness off him and give it to me! Something did happen. I felt a huge surge of heat and energy passing through my hands and Matthew felt

Falling in Love

the same surge entering his head. I believe that we experienced one of those rare moments of Divine Healing.

Matthew gradually improved. Eventually he broke through his barrier and discovered the cause of his darkness. As a child he had been anally and orally raped by a neighbour, a soldier. The experience was so bad for Matthew that he had blocked it from his mind completely. In fact, he was so successful at the mental block that he had actually been treated for polio instead of post-traumatic stress, a condition not known about at the time.

Matthew has become very well. He is now happily married and is a good dad. He is very successful in his working life. He may feel the odd twinge of mental pain, but we all feel that as we go through life.

Matthew's sufferings brought me very close to him. I held him in my arms at his bad times. I often held his hand or hugged him. And we slept together a great deal, something we both wanted to do. When he stayed in my house he often asked, "Do you mind if I sleep in your bed tonight? It makes me feel very safe." We just put our arms around each other and slept. Sometimes I found this very hard to do. After all, I was gay and attracted to Matthew. But he needed my love and there was no way I was going to hurt him by overstepping any boundary. One night in bed he did ask me, "Pat, did you ever kiss a man?" I said "No." "Maybe it's just as well," he said, "It mightn't stop at a kiss!" I thought about that a lot. But there was no way I was ever going to hurt Matthew or compromise his emotional or mental health. Love often involves saying "yes" to ourselves and others. But sometimes real love demands we say "no" to ourselves. That's why love is often so painful. God has been quite good to me in giving me the strength to say "no" to myself when it was appropriate to do so.

I MET "TIMMY" WHEN I WAS in my late twenties and he was in his early twenties. He knew me as a priest and I gradually got to know him. He was married, handsome, intelligent and greatly troubled. He had every reason to be troubled. His beautiful young wife was ill and there was every possibility that he could lose her. One of his children was also ill and while the child was not in danger of death she could never be cured. All this illness, together with a great inner darkness (possibly inherited) brought Timmy to the very edge of despair — to doctors, to prescribed drugs, to panic attacks and to thoughts of suicide. It was all perfectly understandable. Such troubles would bring most of us to a similar place.

I had my own dark cloud. I was very lonely too. I was leading a very busy life as a priest and had an awful lot of pressures weighing me down. I was more or less in denial about my sexuality, running away from it through fear and guilt. Timmy and I met under our two dark clouds and we bonded. We spent a lot of time together talking and walking and sometimes crying.

Our friendship became intense. Like Matthew and I, we would often sleep together. It was non-sexual, especially for Timmy. He was fully heterosexual. But he seemed to need and appreciate the love and affection of an understanding male friend. It was difficult for me. Looking back, I'm sure that Timmy must have guessed I was gay. I'm sorry now I didn't tell him. It would have been a great relief. Eventually I found sleeping with him too difficult to do. I told him so but didn't tell him the reason. He must have known. So we would lie together a while and then sleep separately, often in the same room. Eventually I was moved from Belfast and over time the distance affected our intimacy. But I think that intimacy was affected anyway by the pain, for me, of hiding my full feelings for Timmy.

Timmy is a very good man. In difficult circumstances he has been a faithful husband and father. He has had to battle with anxiety and despair for years. He is deeply spiritual. It is the most natural thing in the world to admire and love someone like that.

MEN'S NEED TO BOND EMOTIONALLY with other men is, to my mind, a sadly neglected need. I am socially very liberal but I see the immense value of the stable family with children experiencing the love of both a mother and a father. Traditionally, we tend think of the father bonding with his daughters and the mother bonding with her sons. And of course that's wonderful. But the fathers and sons, and mothers and daughters, need to bond too.

I have met a lot of men in my life and ministry who never bonded with their fathers and that lack of bonding left them with great regrets and sadness, and sometimes even left them emotionally damaged. I have often stood by a graveside, having said the final prayers over the father of a family, and a tearful son has said, "I did love him but I never told him."

I have never really felt any desire to be married — for obvious reasons — but even if I had I would have been very scared of the huge responsibility of being a Dad. If fathers are not sensitive and aware they can, mainly through inhibition, leave an awful lot of loving undone and even do a fair share of emotional harm to their children, particularly their sons, because I think the gulf between fathers and sons is generally wider than that between fathers and daughters.

It is very sad that men seem to be able to bond, hug and exchange affectionate kisses only when euphoric at football matches or drunk out of their minds in pubs!

HENRY DAVID THOREAU SAID: "Every man is the builder of a temple, called his body, to the God he worships, after a style purely his own, nor can he get off by hammering marble instead. We are all sculptors and painters, and our material is our own flesh and blood and bones."

I believe that the teenage experimentation with sex that most people go through is both natural and good and the fact that I missed out on that phase was not healthy or good for me. It contributed to and indeed compounded my sense of repression, fear and guilt. Later in life, I was to have a few very short but very intense relationships — the equivalent perhaps of the "teenage crushes" or "first loves" I did not allow myself to have earlier in my life. I got so much from these relationships and feel free enough in my faith today, that rather than running off to confession about them, I instead thank God for them.

"Darren" was an angel of liberation who was allowed to enter my life. He was in his late twenties and is gay. He is more than six foot tall, dark and very handsome. He has a master's degree from university. He is a good communicator and is very at ease with his sexuality. He and I spent some special times together. It was very relaxing, freeing and deeply spiritually touching. We would always meet at his place. He would prepare the room by pulling the curtains and creating soft lighting. He would light candles and play music. We would talk for a long time — about him and about me. From the beginning, he knew who I was. He told me that my public "coming out" had helped him to come out to members of his family. He was warm and friendly and affectionate. I opened up and talked freely to Darren. We sometimes went for meals together.

It was clear to both of us from the beginning that we were not meeting to have a long-term relationship. I was lonely, he was lonely. I found him attractive and he wanted to spend special time with a mature man. We exchanged huge physical affection — many hugs and many kisses. He always gave me an unhurried full-body massage. While it was happening I just closed my eyes and relaxed. As the massage progressed, I felt relieved of all tensions and pressures. It was both special and therapeutic not to have to hide my sexuality and body and to be with someone who was not hiding their sexuality and body either. At the end of the massage, I felt totally drained of all negative energies and totally at ease.

We still keep in touch. Could I have fallen in love with him completely? Of course I could; but he could not have settled for me forever. But I will always treasure our times together and how our loving affection allowed me to "walk the walk" and not just "talk the talk", helping me to free myself up humanly, sexually and spiritually. I knew that I could not hold onto the gift forever. But for me, a man shakily making his way from total repression towards freedom, it was "better to have loved and lost than never to have loved at all".

"GARETH" TOO WAS IN HIS LATE TWENTIES and is a primary school teacher. Like Darren he is gay and is from rural Ireland. We met on a journey between Scotland and Ireland, clicked immediately, chatted the whole trip and agreed to get in touch.

Gareth lived in a very dimly lit room in Belfast and whenever I visited him always had very relaxing music playing in the background. He was a part-time aromatherapist and introduced me to the relaxation and healing powers of aromatherapy oils. He and I always talked a lot and again I found pleasure, peace, freedom and the escape of repression, fear and guilt. During my times with Gareth my head emptied of many years' worth of negative thoughts and hang-ups.

Afterwards we would go for a meal and long chats. We became friends but again we both knew from the beginning that we were not destined to be life partners. We were always kind and helpful to each other. Eventually he moved to Scotland and sadly we lost touch. How lovely it was to be able to be myself and to be so totally accepted by another human being as myself — Catholic, priest and all!

In fact I had a most wonderful spiritual experience with Gareth, an experience I can only call a revelation or a vision. While with him I felt transported to another level. Suddenly I had a vision of the crucified Christ returning to Heaven to the Godhead, in between the crucifixion and the resurrection. In the vision I saw God the "Father" with woman's breasts. He/She was breastfeeding Christ and putting the milk of life back into his pale, bloodless and wounded body. I later described this vision to an artist friend who painted it. He has never really been able to display the painting. The few people he has shown it to laugh out of nervousness or get very angry at what they see as "blasphemy".

This vision was most extraordinary. I had been used to thinking of people getting visions in a church or maybe even in the stark quiet of a monk's cell. But to be having a vision in the context of an intimate encounter, through physical and sexual pleasure, brought home to me very strongly that God is as present in our bedrooms as He is in our cathedrals. In fact, he must be very present in bedrooms, as that is where most conceptions take place, with men and women acting as

His "pro-creators" and with the infusion of the human soul by God taking place at conception.

It also taught me that sexual intimacy was not a bad or evil thing if one could be so profoundly touched by God at such a sexual moment. For me, the vision was a grant of Divine Affirmation in my very connected sexuality and spirituality.

WHEN I FIRST MET "ANDREW" I hardly gave him a second glance. He was in his early twenties. I did not think he was especially attractive. It stayed that way for a while as we met casually and socially. But something clicked. It started with a knowing and recognising glance. Eventually we plumbed the very depths of each other's souls. We fell in love.

We had hours together when we talked, had a meal and a drink and went for walks. We had occasional afternoons or evenings together. We had fewer nights together but a small number of nights were "stolen". We had to be discreet, for various reasons.

We soon discovered two vital things. Andrew discovered that I was very sexually repressed and inexperienced. In spite of his young age, he was very experienced and he became a sort of "professor of sensuality" for me. I don't mean lustful sex; we bonded emotionally very deeply.

But I discovered that Andrew had never really been deeply loved. He had never received all the love and affection that every human being needs to be emotionally healthy. In fact a lot of the attention he had received as a child and young adult was violent attention. And I was able to introduce Andrew to love, affection, warmth, emotional expression. He responded so enthusiastically.

We had a very special friendship that lasted for several months until circumstances parted us. I would have wanted him to be a lifetime partner, but so many things were in the way that made it impossible. Our time together had to come to an end.

FOR SIXTEEN YEARS, FROM 1984 UNTIL 2000, I had a "secret love" and to this day he is a special friend. When I met "David" in 1984 he was eighteen and I was thirty-two. He was a very sensitive lad and came from a family with many health and social problems. He was and is very intelligent but for a number of complex reasons he has always found social situations very intimidating. But when he is comfortable he is extremely articulate, knowledgeable and very good company. He is widely read and very talented. He is an excellent cook and a better-than-average DIY man. We have always enjoyed each other's company and of course like all people who are close we have had our rows and battles. We are both strong-willed and opinionated.

I met David at a time of crisis. Things were not going well in his home and he was more or less holed up in his room. His mother came to see me in distress and asked me to help. It was late at night and I thought that I might solve the problem, even temporarily, by telephoning and arranging a proper chat the next day. I rang the house and David answered. He literally told me to "fuck off". When I threatened to come out after him he dared me to and told me that he would have the police remove me. My dander was up and out I went.

It took me quite a while to talk my way into his room. Eventually he let me in and he treated me to scorn and sarcasm. I asked him to come for a little drive and he agreed. We talked a little and arranged to meet the next day and I left him home.

We kept in touch. David began calling to see me. Eventually he asked if he could study in my house as it was quieter than home. He did that. After a while he began to stay the occasional night. Then he stayed a lot of nights. Finally he moved in. But he always maintained his room at home.

Eventually we developed an intimate and a sexual relationship. I was the initiator of that intimacy. In the beginning, I felt the old guilt and rushed off to confession. But as love grew — and love did grow — the guilt evaporated and for the first time in my life I felt free to love without guilt.

I certainly enjoyed our physical intimacy. I enjoyed the friendship and the companionship. I enjoyed all our conversations. We went for walks and for meals. We had some wonderful holidays — Israel, Egypt, France, Belgium, the Netherlands, Spain. I also enjoyed, for the first time, having my own special person in my life. I was no longer alone and that made me so very happy.

I'm sure I was not an easy person to be with. I am very headstrong and pretty dominant. David is a reserved, private person and I am outgoing. He found it increasingly hard to be out with me in public. He hated it when we were out and we would hear a whisper, "There's yer man Buckley." He often walked a few feet behind me in public. Yet he was interested in all my efforts, controversies and battles. He didn't always agree with me. In fact, he increasingly challenged me and disagreed with me. But he was always there as core support.

Looking back now, I think that I can analyse the dynamic of our relationship fairly objectively. We were the very best of friends — and still are. We were lovers. We were partners. I always say to David (but he disagrees) that I wielded a fairly direct power over him and that he wielded a very successful manipulative power over me. But I think that there might have been too much of the parent/child dynamic in our relationship. This was probably because of the age difference and because of our different personalities. But this is not unusual. Many partnerships and marriages have a similar underlying dynamic. Many husbands want a wife to be part-wife, part-mother. Many wives want a husband to be part-husband, part-protective daddy.

As the years went past, David and I had a few big disagreements. There was one in particular, where we both saw a particular situation in a very different light. We could not agree and we could not even agree to differ. That did some damage to our relationship. In hindsight, I also realise that David had perhaps begun to develop, that the parent/child dynamic was just not working as it had. And I found it hard to readjust. I was perhaps, too possessive, though of course David had his own selfishnesses. So our partnership gradually changed into a non-sexual friendship. It happened very gradually and seemed to be a natural progression.

For a few years David had known another man and had developed quite a friendship with him. In November of 2000 they decided to set up home together. I wished them well, but I was very sad the day David finally left. I tried to keep busy. I then tried to ignore his going. But when he left and I heard the click of the door behind him I broke down and sobbed uncontrollably. I knew that I was going to see him a lot and be in touch most days but the going was very difficult. It was the end of a sixteen-year era.

MY SADNESS OVER DAVID'S DEPARTURE only lasted a few days before I was hit with another sadness. Nero, my twelve-year-old Doberman, whom I had had since he was a six-week-old puppy, got a terminal spinal problem and had to be put to sleep. The vet came to the house. I had been massaging Nero for an hour and he was thoroughly relaxed. The vet put the needle in Nero's leg, having shaved a little spot, and injected the lethal substance. Nero gave a little sigh and stopped breathing. His body went limp and his bladder emptied. He was gone. I was on my knees. My tears were falling down on Nero's black and tan coat. My pal of twelve years was gone. I buried him in my garden and erected a little plaque in his memory. I had received so much love and affection from Nero.

It was tough to be losing David and Nero in the one week. I asked myself, "What is this time of loss all about?" Some years ago in counselling and therapy I had told the therapist that when I was worried about anything I always had disturbing dreams about something happening to David, Nero or my mother — obviously the three emotional pillars of my life. In a week, two of those three pillars had been swept away. I was paralysed by a sense of loss. I cried a lot. But in the sadness I was able to joke with my mother and ask her to mind herself!

David and I will always be friends. Our sixteen years together created a bond. I thank God for our relationship. I care for him greatly and wish him every possible happiness and good fortune in the future and in his new relationship.

AT THE BEGINNING OF AN EARLIER CHAPTER I quoted Dag Hammarskjöld, the second Secretary General of the United Nations who died in a plane crash in 1961 while on a peace mission to the Congo. Hammarskjöld said: "Pray that your loneliness may spur you into finding something to live for, great enough to die for."

Most of us suffer loneliness to a greater or lesser degree. How we manage our loneliness is so very important. Loneliness breaks some people completely. Some people commit suicide because they can no longer stand their loneliness. Other people try to kill the pain of their loneliness with alcohol or drugs. Others still allow their loneliness to drive them into loveless and abusive relationships and marriages. Some people cope with their loneliness by becoming workaholics.

Dag Hammarskjöld is absolutely correct when he says that we have to approach our loneliness from a very positive perspective and instead of letting it get us down or defeating us, we should use our loneliness to spur us into action to do something good and special with our lives.

I believe that the spiritual and human value of suffering and loneliness is one of the most intense forms of human experience. I believe that suffering has incalculable value because God used suffering (His son's) to redeem mankind, and God uses only the best of ways, and because most of the important good things that have ever been achieved in the history of mankind have been achieved through human suffering. I believe that our suffering, if we don't let it make us bitter, makes us acutely conscious of how small and insignificant we are in the context of creation, the universe and existence. It opens a huge spiritual vista to us and makes us rely on God or "the other" and not on ourselves with our narrowness of vision and our powerlessness. I believe that our suffering makes us incredibly compassionate to others, especially to others who are suffering in any way.

None of us wants to suffer or be lonely. Yet I believe that suffering is a great mystery — in the positive sense. When I look back on my life and see the moments that I was very lonely, suffering or in some other great pain, I can also see that they were moments and times that were truly cathartic. They were crossroads through which I went on to better and greater things and through which my life changed for the better.

Let me give a few examples. If I had not been expelled from Clonliffe College in 1973, something I regarded at the time as an absolute disaster, I would never have experienced three wonderful years in St John's College, Waterford, nor would I have known the wonderful people I met there. Neither would I have ended up in Wales as a priest for two years nor have had the immensely enriching, if painful, experiences I had there.

If Cardinal Cahal Daly had not done me the grave injustice of "sacking" me from my parish in 1986, I would not have had the last wonderful eighteen years of my life with their breathtaking diversity and rewarding independence. I would be an ordinary rule-bound parish priest, plodding through long boring routines and would not have been able to minister to the thousands of alienated and hurt people I have had the privilege of serving.

My loneliness, suffering, and everything else that's inside me spurs me on to live for life, for God, for others and for the self that I now appreciate and love. And that would be enough to die for too!

TODAY I AM STILL LONELY but I now know that I am lonely because I am missing one thing in my life — the love and companionship of a life partner. I feel, at this stage of my life, that it is not good for me to be alone.

I would like to have a partner and a life companion. Everyday I pray about this to God. I say to Him: "Lord, more than anything else in my life I want to do your will. If it is your will that I am to be alone and lonely then I accept your will and just ask you to give me the strength to bear that loneliness and pain. But if it is not against your will, Lord, I ask you to lead me to the person of my destiny."

To such a companion I would give my very all. But I also need to receive — love, affection, understanding, encouragement, sensuality. I don't want to wake up at three o'clock in the morning alone in a bed anymore. I want someone there to put an arm around, or who I can watch sleeping and give thanks to God for them. I don't want to go on holidays alone again. I don't want to sit alone or in a group in a restaurant and benignly envy couples in love at other tables. I want to see someone looking at me the way the couples whose marriages I celebrate look at each other. At this stage of my life — my human life and my spiritual life — I know that I need an "other" to complement my "me". I want my human loneliness to end, or to at least be tempered, by the presence in my life of a humanly and spiritually compatible partner.

AS WELL AS GREAT JOY and happiness, love often involves pain. We must always hope for the joy and always be ready for the pain. Sometimes love involves loss, separation and letting go. This experience can be so utterly devastating.

We need to communicate our love. If we love someone we should never take them for granted. We should show them with our lives and actions that we love them. But we all need to hear the one we love tell us that they love us. I was once in a relationship in which the other party was very undemonstrative and hardly ever told me they loved me. They always used the excuse: "Sure you know I love you. I don't have to tell you." I found this terribly painful, mind-blowing in fact, and protested in verse:

You Know I Love You

"You know I love you.
I don't need to tell you."

Yes, I know you love me.
But my heart needs to hear you say it.

> "I'm not the expressive type.
> I'm not from an expressive family."
>
> I understand that.
> But I need you to make me the exception.
>
> "I'm not touchy-feely.
> But I do have deep feelings."
>
> I'm aware of that.
> But my every fibre craves your touch.
>
> "I've always just had sex.
> Making love scares me; I don't know how."
>
> I can feel that in your body.
> Let me tenderly lead you.
>
> "You have me tense, afraid, confused.
> My tummy churns."
>
> I know you are churning.
> Let us churn together —
> Love's sweet, salty butter.

WHEN I WAS A TWENTY-YEAR-OLD seminarian who thought he knew everything but who really knew so little, a nun in Dublin said to me one day: "You'll never be a good priest until you have fallen in love with another human being".

Full to the brim of adolescent religious crap and of the absolute certainty that comes from ignorance and inexperience, I arrogantly wrote that nun off as a neurotic and menopausal creature who was coming to regret never having had sex and babies. When I later discovered that she had served on the missions and had had a long and passionate relationship with a priest I further wrote her off as prejudiced — transferring her own issues onto me.

But of course she was perfectly right and I was pathetically ignorant and stupid — in my seminarian's black suit, white shirt and black tie and my "certainty" about my future chastity and celibacy. For as the Bible reminds us: "If you cannot love the brother you can see how can you ever hope to love the God you cannot see?" And if we do not experience loving and being loved here below how can we ever really believe in and experience loving and being loved from above?

How can someone who never knew their father or who had a bad father ever properly comprehend God as their loving father? How could someone whose mother abandoned them or who had a "bad" mother ever appreciate the loving motherhood of God? An only child is at a disadvantage trying to understand that everyone else in the world is his or her "brother" or "sister".

How can someone who never heard a human being say to them "I love you" imagine what it would be like to have God whisper that into their heart? How can someone who has never held another person in their arms and whispered "I love you" feel what it is like to truly embrace God and whisper "I love you"?

In the movie *Oh God!* the atheist (John Denver) asks God (George Burns), "What are you doing about all the suffering in the world?" God answers, "What am I doing about it? I have given you each other, haven't I?" There is so much wisdom in that statement. God has given us each other. We have each other to practise love on. We learn to love God after many years and decades of practising to love each other. We truly come to know God's love for us when true love, real love, has been mediated to us through and by another human being.

Over the years I have often quoted in my sermons that wisdom-packed verse:

> I sought my God and my God I could not see;
> I sought my soul and my soul eluded me;
> I sought my brother — and I found all three.

I am not saying that it is impossible for a person who has never experienced human love not to have a relationship with God. God and grace are far more than capable of bypassing all human channels. But God only bypasses the human by way of exception. When He wanted to send His Son into the world He did not send Him out of the sky and as a prince on a fiery chariot. He sent him into an ordinary womb

Falling in Love

and an ordinary family. And when God wanted to save the world He did it through His Son being accused, arrested, tortured, tried, convicted and killed.

God's approaches to us have always been achieved through our human experience rather than through non-worldly signs and wonders. If God wants us to know all about love, and love is the most important issue on God's agenda, He is going to mediate that knowledge and experience to us through the human too. In saying that I'm not saying that God never communicates directly with us. Of course He does. I have experienced it personally. What I am saying is that, as a rule, God uses His creation to mediate all things, including and especially His love.

I have only had one "spectacular" experience of God touching me through the physical presence of another — the "vision" I had while with my friend Gareth. But on many occasions, while in the physical presence of another human being, I have felt in the physical presence of God. While naked and unashamed before another loving human being, I have felt naked and unashamed before God. While being held in a loving embrace by another human being I have felt myself to be in the loving embrace of God. While being caressed by another human being who was making me feel secure and attached and un-alone, I felt that God was caressing me and making me feel secure, attached to Him and absolutely un-alone. The Divine Kiss was implicit in the human kiss; the Divine Ecstasy was implicit in the human ecstasy; the Divine Bonding was implicit in the human bonding; the Divine Resolution was implicit in the human resolution. And afterwards God was also there in the quietening of the breathings, the slowing of the heartbeats, the fallings asleep intertwined, the all-night-long semiconscious pleasure of two being one, the awakening to find oneself not alone, the long lingering breakfast, the pre-separation shower and the many times over following days and nights sensing the beloved's scents on pillows you never wish to change.

On a number of occasions, people I have shared a night with have asked me in the morning: "Did you have your hand on my head during the night? What were you doing? Were you praying?" The answer is, yes, I was praying. I was thanking God for the beauty of another human being and all the beautiful things about them. I was thanking God for the love and pleasure we had shared and for how I had found God and His love in that love and pleasure. And I was asking God to send His Spirit and His angels into my companion's heart and life and bless them in every possible way.

It Happens All the Time in Heaven
(Hafiz)

It happens all the time in heaven,
And some day

It will begin to happen
Again on earth —

That men and women who are married,
And men and men who are
Lovers,

And women and women
Who give each other
Light,

Often will get down on their knees

And while tenderly
Holding their lover's hand,

With tears in their eyes,

Will sincerely speak, saying,

"My Dear,
How can I be more loving to you;

How can I be more
Kind?"

Pat, on Granny's knee, 1953

Pat driving his first car, 1955!

First day at school: Pat and his sister Margaret in Carlow, 1956

Pat and Margaret on their First Holy Communion Day, Carlow, 1958

Pat and Margaret with cousin Yvonne Joyce, her mother Peg and her father-in-law, Ciaran

Pat, as adolescent and "third parent", with younger brothers John (12) and Alan outside their house in Ballymun, late 1960s

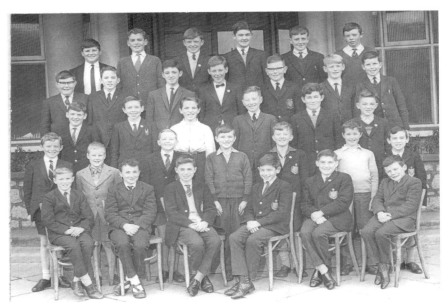

School picture, St Canice's CBS, Dublin, 1964; Pat, aged 12, is in the second row from the back, third from right

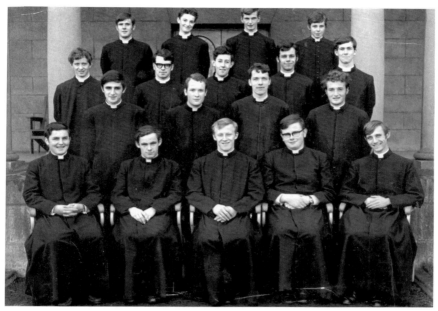

First day in Clonliffe seminary, 1970;
Pat, aged 18, is second from right in the front row

Lourdes, 1972, with
Brother Gerard RIP

As a Legion of Mary
"missionary", Glasgow, 1972

Ordination class, Waterford, 1974; Pat, aged 22, is in the back row on the right

Ordination portrait, June 1976

First Mass with the Buckley family, Ballymun, Dublin, 7 June 1976

Pat with Rosie, Belfast, 1979

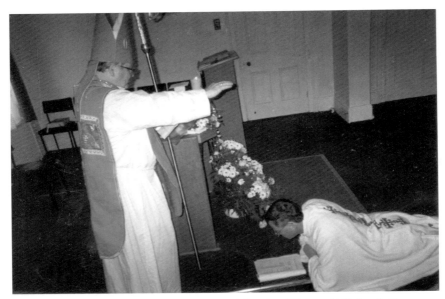

Consecration of Bishop Pat Buckley by Bishop Michael Cox,
at The Oratory, Larne, 19 May 1998

Pat, with his mother, following
his consecration as Bishop

Bishop Pat Buckley's
Episcopal coat of arms:
Tolerance, Love, Diversity

"Coming out" in *The News of the World* on 10 October 1999

"Rocking the boat": cartoon by Eamonn F. Murphy, 2000

Bishop Pat Buckley in reflective mood, 1999

Pat in The Oratory at Prince's Gardens,
Larne, County Antrim, in spring 2005

Chapter Seven

"Coming Out"

"The Sacrament of 'Coming Out' is a kind of letting go; a letting go of the images of personhood, sexuality and selfhood that society has put on one in favour of trusting oneself enough to let oneself be oneself. This emptying and letting go is a school of wisdom, a theology of the apophatic God, the God of darkness whom the straight world needs to hear more about" — Fr Matthew Fox

AS MY LIFE PROGRESSED I grew more and more tired of carrying my great sexual secret. I also felt increasingly "dishonest". Not that I was telling a lot of lies about it; I wasn't. Rather, there seemed to be two "me's". There was the "me" that people thought I was. And there was the real and full me. I was getting to the stage where I wanted the whole me, the real me, to be known. Of course, people with public profiles are entitled to a private life. I believe that, like everyone else, I am entitled to a great degree of privacy. But for a priest, even a controversial one, who has a duty to and is expected to speak out about things like sexuality, I believe it is necessary to nail one's own colours to the mast.

I was also doing more and more work with the gay, lesbian, bisexual and transgendered community — counselling, talks, gay blessings and so on. I have never had anything but compassion for all these people and they always knew it. But I felt that they too had a right to know that I was a member of their community myself. Even if they didn't have that "right", I wanted to let them know who I truly was so that they might experience an even greater solidarity with me.

My plan was simple but, I think, courageous enough. I was going to finish my counselling, be properly "grounded", have integrated my sexuality and my spirituality and write my book — this book! I did begin to write the book. However, I was not to be allowed the luxury of "outing" myself in my own way and my own time.

My good and loyal friend John Moore, the Bureau Chief of the Irish *News of the World*, telephoned me to say that there was a story going around journalistic circles that I was gay. Apparently two young men had approached the Sunday newspapers in Belfast with some "evidence" that I was gay. They were looking for money and were playing off newspaper against newspaper. To this day I do not know for certain who those two young men were, but I have strong suspicions. Nor indeed do I know what "evidence" they had for their story. I think they had little or nothing apart from the fact that they were former "friends" in whom I had foolishly placed my trust. But I realised that, as they say, "the word was on the street". I have always said that if stories are to be told about me, I want to be the teller myself.

I kept my ear to the journalistic ground. Nothing happened, but I knew that it was only a matter of time. There was no way I was going to live in fear and trepidation about my sexuality after all I had been through about it. So I made a decision that, all arrogance aside, was a brave and a wise decision. I decided that I would tell my family and immediate parishioners that I was gay and that I would then make it public myself. I chose to use my regular Sunday column in the *News of the World* as my forum for "coming out".

I was concerned about my mother. I wanted to tell her first. She loves the shrine of Mary at Lourdes in France. I decided that I would bring her there to tell her. One morning in the Jeanne d'Arc Hotel in Lourdes, we sat and sipped coffee and I told her. She was not overly surprised and not at all perturbed. I think that mothers know things instinctively. She is a bit of a nervous traveller, so we shared a large hotel room. That night we were in bed with the lights off. She called over, "Are you asleep?" I answered, "No." She said, "I'm just thinking that I never thought that I could love you more than I did. But tonight I do." A mother's love at its best is always unconditional love.

I arrived back from Lourdes on the Friday and rendezvoused with John Moore of the *News of the World* and our photographer at a Dublin hotel. I sat with John — as much a friend as a journalist — and told him my story. He was as sensitive and sympathetic as he is to everyone. We took some photographs. I stayed overnight in a Dublin hotel and met our photographer early the next morning. We went to Sandymount Strand and took some more photographs of me walking alone on the beach. Sunday's headline was: "Why I Want the World to Know I'm Gay."

I had a very restless night's sleep on the Saturday night. *If I'm lucky*, I thought, *I will get fifty per cent acceptance and fifty per cent rejection*. I was afraid. Baring one's soul publicly is never easy. Making such a public general confession is even more difficult.

The day the article appeared, the telephone calls and the letters started arriving. I was astounded. I was receiving ninety-nine per cent love, compassion and acceptance. Many of the calls and letters just thanked me for being honest. I was moved to tears.

I had one worry. The following Saturday, I had a big wedding ceremony in Roscommon. It would be my first time to say Mass and perform a big wedding after publicly announcing that I was gay. The couple I was marrying were also worried. One of them had been divorced and they had a difficult enough time getting their families used to divorce and remarriage without the added controversy or "problem" of their wedding celebrant being a newly publicly confessed gay bishop. I went to Roscommon in some fear and trepidation. But I needn't have worried. Everyone was wonderful and kind. Just before the wedding started a large red-faced farmer in his eighties with big rough hands took my hand between his two and told me, "I'm delighted to meet an honest man." That was very moving.

SINCE COMING OUT I HAVE HAD very few problems with homophobia. Of course there are ignorant homophobes about and I've had some problems. For example, the Christmas after I came out I was having a drink with two friends in the lobby of a Belfast hotel. There was a Christmas party in the adjoining function room. A young man came out of the function a few times and called me a "fucking queer". He was drunk and I decided to ignore him, hoping that he would get bored. But he didn't. He persisted. So I approached the manager, told him my problem and asked him to eject the young man from his hotel. The manager failed to act, so I called the nearest police station. Several policemen arrived within minutes. The police and I entered the function room where hundreds were partying. The young abuser was on the dance floor with a beer bottle in his hand. I pointed him out. The police removed him from the function, made him apologise to me and brought him home. I later wrote to the managing director of the hotel group to complain about the manager's inaction. He wrote me an angry and unsympathetic reply. I made my hotel protest not only on my own behalf but on behalf of all the gay people who take abuse everyday and who for whatever reason cannot fight back.

More recently, in 2001, some building work was being done beside my local bank. On several occasions, when I was going to do my banking, the dozen or so building workers called me names. I would overhear words like "queer" and "puff". I decided not to react, hoping that it might just cease. But it only got worse. One Monday I went to the bank and got some jeering on the way in. I decided that that would be the day when I would sort these guys out. On the way out of the bank, one of the workers shouted a joke to the others: "Did you hear about the two queer ghosts . . .?" I stopped and looked at the top of the scaffolding at the ignoramus who was mouthing. I said to him: "Would you like to come down here and repeat that to me?" "I'd love to," he said. Down he came and repeated his homophobic joke. I was angry. Amongst other things, I told him, "People like you who are ignorant, bigoted and prejudiced, and who mouth about other people's sexual orientation generally have a major sex problem themselves!" He was looking at me with a mixture of anger and stupidity as I got out my mobile phone and dialled for the police. The police arrived and took down their names and warned that harassment was now a prosecutable offence. The following morning a senior bank manager informed me that the ringleader of the abuse was no longer with them and apologised profusely. Afterwards, when I passed the building site there wasn't a word. I will not allow myself to be abused in the street. I believe that all forms of "queer bashing", whether actual or subtle should be forcefully resisted. Again, I made my protest on behalf not only of myself but on behalf of all the gay people who suffer taunts and cannot answer back.

On one occasion I was physically assaulted on the street. It was Christmas Eve 2000. I was doing my last-minute Christmas shopping on the streets of Larne where I live. I was passing a pub/restaurant. As I walked on the other side of the street, a bouncer at the bar started shouting homophobic abuse. I walked straight over to him, looked him in the eyes and said: "I will not take verbal abuse from anyone in the street and especially not from a monkey like you." He grabbed me by the neck, hard enough to make it difficult for me to breathe, and then banged my whole body up against a pub menu sign. Again, I took out my mobile phone and sent for the police. They arrived and took details from both myself and my assailant. A police investigation began. My assailant managed to find four witnesses, from within the pub, who told the police that he had never touched me! I of course had no witnesses to prove that he did. Plenty of members of the public saw him hitting me but of course they were afraid to come forward. So the case was never brought to court. My assailant has since gone on to verbally abuse me on the street on a number of occasions and most recently was cautioned by the police for harassment.

I was saddened and shocked recently to visit a gay couple living in the heart of rural Northern Ireland who have to keep closed-circuit cameras at the back and front of their pretty cottage to try to catch people who smash up their property, empty their bins all over their garden and shout abuse as they pass.

I HAD ALWAYS MINISTERED COMPASSIONATELY to the gay, lesbian, bisexual and transgender community. Because of my own inner struggle I had a very immediate and innate understanding of the struggle of those with a "minority" sexual orientation. But in coming out I firmly nailed my colours to the mast and that increased my credibility and relevance to the gay community.

Over the past few years I have helped conduct spiritual workshops for gay and lesbian people in Dublin, Belfast and Derry. I hope to begin a monthly non-denominational Eucharistic service in Belfast soon for the gay and lesbian community and their family and friends and indeed for all who want to attend.

One of my strongest convictions is that the gay community, having been rejected by mainstream Christianity, should not believe that God has rejected them but should, in response, create their own theology, spirituality and morality.

In the early 1980s I wrote the following verse:

My Sexuality

My sexuality,
Source of joy, pleasure.
Motivation of my life,
Cause of the many good things I do.

Also source of pain,
Sometimes frustration,
Also sin.

We must live with
Contradictions;
Knowing that if we live with them,
We shall be saved,
In spite of them,
Maybe even,
Because of them!

In 2002 I presented a discussion paper to the Belfast spirituality group. I will finish this chapter by repeating some of the points of discussion from that paper that related to sexuality.

The Bible does not address, much less condemn, the phenomenon of two people of the same sex living a life of committed love together. Men and women had not really looked closely at this notion two thousand, or five thousand years ago. The Bible condemns things like the sodomising of defeated military enemies, male pagan temple prostitution and straight men having "fun" sex together.

The Gospel of St John says that wherever there is love there is God. This means that God is both present and revealed in same-sex love. The body is as good as the soul. It is created by God. We Christians believe in the resurrection of the body as well as of the soul. So the body must be as good as the soul if it is fit to exist in Heaven for all eternity.

Sex is good. It is God's gift. It even allows men and women to share in God's role as Creator. That's why we pro-create. Sex is only wrong, immoral and sinful if it hurts someone or if it is used to use or abuse. A sexually active life (in love) is as pleasing in God's sight as celibacy/virginity.

Homophobia is an evil. It is both immoral and sinful. HIV and AIDS is a human illness like any other. It is not God's wrath. What kind of God would wage biological warfare on his children?

Gay and lesbian people will be as welcome in Heaven as all others. As spiritual people, gay and lesbian people are invited to have faith and to pray and worship as they see fit. Gay and lesbian people should develop and distribute their own spirituality, theology and worship.

I finished the discussion with the Belfast group by suggesting the following "gay commandments"; I would, however, suggest that these are as relevant to heterosexuals as homosexuals:

1. I am the Lord your God. You shall not have strange gods before me — neither idols nor material things nor people.

2. You shall not use your gift of speech to hurt another brother or sister.

3. You shall keep every day holy by being spiritual and by being kind to others. You shall not harm your body by the use of alcohol or drugs.

4. You shall honour and treasure all your family and other relationships.

5. You shall not hurt another either physically, verbally, sexually or mentally. In My Kingdom, human flesh is not "meat" and young people are not "chickens".

6. You shall use your sexuality in the context of love and never to hurt, use or abuse.

7. You shall be honest in all your dealings. Never make a date and stand someone up.

8. You shall not lie, bear false witness or backbite another. Avoid the bitchiness of some members of the gay community.

9. You shall not be controlled by jealousy or envy. You shall not come between a couple.

10. You shall do all the good you can for as long as you can.

Part Two

Towards a New Spirituality of Sex

Chapter Eight

THE CATHOLIC CHURCH: SEX, LIES AND GUILT

"The man sitting across from me was a member of the American hierarchy, but the only hint of his office was the modest Episcopal ring on his right hand. We spoke for a long time about the priesthood and the church. After a brief lull in the conversation, he shattered the silence with a quiet reflection, almost as if he were talking to himself;
'The thing that pains me about the organisation to which
I belong is that it is rotten from the top down'."
— *Richard Sipe, US priest and psychotherapist*

RICHARD SIPE SAYS that this American bishop was objecting to "the rottenness of secrecy, the misuse of power, the cover-ups, the duplicities to salvage image, and the refusal of the celibate/sexual system to assume responsibility for its behaviours and deficiencies — for itself — for what it truly is". Sipe goes on to make another astounding and alarming statement in the context of child abuse:

> When asked why the American bishops were having such a difficult time dealing with priest sexual abusers, another bishop responded: "Undoubtedly part of the problem is that some of the bishops themselves are abusers."

Richard Sipe's thesis is very straightforward and it is a thesis with which I wholly concur:

> The scandal of priestly sexual abuse of minors, although real and significant in itself, is primarily a symptom of an essentially flawed celibate/sexual system of ecclesiastical power.

Sipe is right when he goes on to say that an analysis of the celibate/ sexual system of the Catholic Church shows that it is based an a false understanding of the nature of human sexuality and primary Christian experience. Sipe is also correct when he states that in two thousand years no Christian church has developed a proper theology and spirituality of sexuality. Sipe reaches a wonderful crescendo when he states:

> Eventually, the church must submit its consideration of sexuality to the realities of evolutionary, molecular, and anthropological biology (that is, scientific perception), along with historical, sociological, and poetic speculation (that is, mystical perception). Failure to take account of scientific discoveries, especially in the areas of physics and biology, renders theological pronouncements on human nature and God uncredible.

These words of Richard Sipe's are nothing short of prophetic. He is correct to assert that the Catholic Church (and indeed the other churches) have not incorporated enough knowledge of physical nature and human sexual nature to have produced an adequate and up-to-date theology of sexuality. This is the heart of the problem and the crisis in the Catholic Church. Our theology and our spirituality are based on erroneous and outdated understandings of God, creation, humanity and sexuality. We need a whole new theology of creation, humanity and sexuality. The old theology is a lie and a lie that is still being taught and preached to the world's billion Catholics — many of whom are not listening.

BISHOPS, PRIESTS, DEACONS, MONKS, religious and lay Catholics have sexually abused children and minors from earliest times. In a second-century commentary on the Bible, Didache says: "Thou shalt not seduce young boys." The Council of Elvira in 309 AD says that the following people should not be given Holy Communion, not even at the point of death: "Bishops, priests and deacons committing a sexual sin" (Canon 18); "Those who sexually abuse boys" (Canon 71); and "People who bring charges against bishops and priests without proving their cases" (Canon 75). Pope Julius III, who presided over the second session of the Council of Trent (1552–1554) entered into a sexual liaison with a fifteen-year-old boy whom he had picked up on the streets of Parma and made him a cardinal before he died in 1555. Jean Jacques Rousseau wrote of the sexual experiences he had at a retreat house in 1725 and of how the religious superiors there thought nothing of it and said it was common among them all.

Of course, we know now of the activities of certain priests and religious in more recent times, both in Ireland and abroad. In December 1993 an independent board of inquiry into activities at the Franciscan Seminary at Santa Barbara in California revealed that twelve of the forty-four priests there had been sexually active with the boys, aged between eleven and seventeen, over a period of twenty-three years. This would mean that 120 boys of the 950 attending in those years had been sexually abused. One of the most notorious examples of a US priest abuser was Fr James Porter of Fall River, Massachusetts. He victimised two hundred minors in the twelve years from 1960 to 1972. His victims spoke of "violent rape, cruel humiliation and sadistic punishment". One priest who actually saw Porter rape a child said to a concerned parishioner: "Father is only human."

In Ireland, there have of course been a large number of high-profile cases of sexual abuse of children by priests and religious, such as Fr Brendan Smyth, Fr Ivan Payne, to whom Cardinal Desmond Connell lent £27,000 to pay off a victim, and Fr Sean Fortune who committed suicide before his trial.

NOT ONLY DO PRIESTS SEDUCE and abuse children. Some priests also seduce vulnerable adults — men and women — who come to them for advice, counselling and spiritual direction.

Currently I co-ordinate a support group in Ireland called Bethany. It consists of 110 women who are or have been in relationships with priests. Six of the women have priests' children. Four have had abortions. In two cases, the priests in question paid for the abortions and travelled with the women to London for their terminations. Some of the women in Bethany are married. Some of the priests involved are having sexual relationships with more than one woman. Very often the woman is only being used and abused.

Some heterosexual priests have told me that the clerical collar is great for "pulling the women". One Belfast curate I knew always referred to his collar as "the bird catcher"! Apparently some women find priests attractive. These women see the priests as kind, fatherlike and sensitive men they can talk to. There is of course also the aspect of the attractiveness of the forbidden fruit.

I recall hearing of a situation from a parish in the Catholic Diocese of Clogher. A young curate, a self-confessed bisexual, fell for a very pretty young married woman and began having an affair with her. She always attended his Masses and always went to communion. The priest would give the Sacred Host to everybody else and say the usual, "Body of Christ." But this woman told me that every time the priest gave her communion, he used to say: "Christ, what a body!" Even I was shocked at that priest's cynicism and blasphemy.

During my priestly life I have encountered a number of priest/nun couples. Recently the Vatican received a report on the abuse of nuns by bishops and priests worldwide. In America this is called "The Third Way" — if you have to be "celibate", have an intimate sexual relationship with a nun! Sometimes these relationships are quite balanced and stable and survive for years and even decades. At other times they are very volatile and great pain is caused all around.

I counselled one woman who was sexually involved with a priest. The priest, who as a member of a religious order had taken a solemn vow of chastity, was not monogamous and had several women in his life. There was a nun whom he described as his "spiritual wife" and he had sexual relationships with at least two other married women. He had "explained" to the woman I was counselling that he could have non-penetrative sex with her; but he could only have penetrative sex with the nun because she and he had agreed a "spiritual marriage". However, he used to ask the other woman to serve his Mass and on one occasion after Mass told her that God wanted her to support him in his ministry by giving him love and sex! This situation was brought to the attention of his religious superiors, who did nothing whatsoever.

This priest and his nun "wife", who are still together, quite regularly go on holidays in cosy little caravans and cottages in out-of-the-way places. The other woman, has, at long last, and on my advice, pulled out of the mad circle and now has much more peace of mind. I don't know if she has been replaced — or indeed what size of team the priest needs today!

I have come across homosexual relationships between priests living together in the same presbytery and lesbian relationships between nuns living in the same convent.

I know of many other situations where priests seduced adults — even in the confessional. In one parish, a religious order priest with vows of poverty, chastity and obedience, visiting to give a mission/retreat was making young women suck his finger through the confessional grille while he masturbated. In another parish a young homosexual male nurse told me that he went for counselling and advice to a young curate. The curate turned off the light in the reception room, placed the young man over the desk and seduced him.

In Belfast I met and had to help a beautiful young woman who had been gang-raped by five priests at a party one evening.

The list of such pastoral abuses is endless.

The other "best kept secret" among the clergy is that many parish housekeepers are the priests' "wives" in all but name. This is a long-standing practice in Ireland and further afield. Over the decades and centuries, many children have resulted. Where else would we get such Irish surnames as McEntaggart (the son of the priest), McEnespie, (the son of the bishop) and McNabb (the son of the abbot)? Love and lust will always find a way!

In recent years, a sixty-year-old priest who was involved in a long-term and loving relationship with a widow used to come to me for confession and spiritual guidance. Talk about the blind leading the blind! One day he said something to me that was so absolutely true. He looked me in the eyes and said: "Pat, they wouldn't let us get rid of our semen and it went to our heads and made us fucking mad." Crude? Not at all. Wise? Perfectly.

GENERALLY I CANNOT BE EASILY SHOCKED — certainly not by sexual matters. But I was shocked by the story a young Irish priest recently told me of his experiences in Rome. He was sent to Rome as a student. He loved Rome itself and its vibrant atmosphere. He also liked the pomp and splendour of the Church in Rome and he was part of many ceremonies there. He was not in the close company of the late Pope himself but he did socialise with people who were extremely close to the Pope and had daily contact with His Holiness.

The young priest is gay — and happily so. He told me stories of the huge amount of gay activity in the seminaries in Rome among the seminarians. He also told me many stories of the sex that takes place between senior clerics, priests, religious and seminarians. Some of the names of those who were and are sexually active in Rome are names we would recognise internationally and in Ireland. This young man wrote a detailed account of his time in Rome, some of which I reproduce here:

> Very early on I was invited to a reception in the Vatican. The centre of attention at this gathering was an aged cardinal; he must have been in his eighties. He was surrounded by adoring seminarians who hung on his every word. This did not surprise me. What did surprise me was the fact that this old man was wearing make-up and behaving in a most flirtatious way with his attentive coterie. The rouge on his face complemented the scarlet of his robes. I remember being shocked, but also intrigued. I wanted to be part of his circle of young admirers.

> The relationships within the seminary were particularly bizarre. Here I was in the place where future bishops were formed. Full of young, handsome, gay men, who knew they were young and handsome, but not so clear about the unmentionable. I had no evidence of gay relationships, but we suspected who might be visiting one another's rooms after lights out. There were a few scenes, quite hilarious in retrospect, when "friends" had a falling out and as a result of too much drink, the beans were spilled in accusation and acrimony.

A few of us knew curial officials, junior monsignors who were on the first rung of the ladders of their ecclesiastical careers. These too showed all the signs of being emotionally boys in the form of men. The Curia — as one insider put it — existed on a sea of bitchery and vindictive gossip. This too could be viewed as being relatively harmless, or maybe not when one considers the power and influence these relatively powerful young men had over the church throughout the world. It was often a boast of some of our curial friends of how they had humiliated some hapless bishop from God-knows-where on his "Ad limina" (five-yearly report visit). The power resided in the junior official, and not the successor of the apostles.

There were also rumours and gossip of higher officials being spotted in gay cruising areas around Rome, or being noticed in Rome's only gay nightclub. The guardians of the Palace Gates, The Swiss Guard, knew the movements of those closest to the top. In such an atmosphere of secrecy and repression, some strange flowers did bloom indeed.

What I experienced day in and day out was a lot of the church and very little of the gospel. In the end I could not maintain the tensions of myself wishing to find expression as an openly gay man, and the option of a covert lifestyle in the corridors of power. The words of a priest helped me to make up my own mind once and for all when he declared: "I would rather be hated for who I am than loved for who I am not."

Is it any wonder then that the American bishop in Richard Sipe's book lamented that his Church was rotten from the top down. Did the late Pope know about these things? I do not know.

Many people will choose not to believe what I have written here. I can do nothing about that. "There are none so blind as those who do not wish to see." But it is the truth. And as Gandhi said: "Even if you are a minority of one, the truth is still the truth."

MANY RECENT STUDIES IN THE US have looked at the extent of the sexual hypocrisy at the heart of the Catholic Church. In a 1992 study by Sheila Murphy, sixty-two per cent of vowed religious said that they were sexually active. In 1993, Fr Andrew Greeley estimated that between two thousand and four thousand US priests were abusing minors. Richard Sipe himself makes many similar claims, based on strong evidence. For instance, in 1976 Sipe concluded that six per cent of American priests were having sex with minors. Ten per cent of priests say that they were propositioned in the seminary. A dozen priests in the US committed suicide between 1990 and 1993 when faced with the exposure of their sexual activity. At least thirty per cent of Catholic priests have a homosexual orientation. One per cent of priests are transvestites. Some priests have encouraged group sex and have organised group sex for teenagers. Only two per cent of priests achieve complete and lifelong celibacy.

The Catholic Church is living and has always lived and taught great lies about sex. While popes, cardinals, bishops and priests have had a merry old time they have tried to make the laity think that they are perfect, sexually pure and that they, the laity, must be chaste and pure also. And as Chaucer said:

> If gold rust, what shall poor iron do?
> For if the priest be foul, in whom we trust,
> What wonder if a layman yield to lust?
> And shame it is, if priest take thought for keep,
> A shitty shepherd, shepherding clean sheep.

THE VAST MAJORITY OF PEOPLE are not suited to celibacy or virginity. It is a charism — a gift from God — but a gift only given to the few. The very first book of the Bible, the Book of Genesis, says "It is not good for man to be alone."

Optional celibacy, as an invitation from God given to the very few, freely and generously embraced, is a wonderfully good thing and frees people up for tremendous love and service. Gandhi was an example. So was Dorothy Day, founder of *The Catholic Worker*. Richard Sipe says: "Celibacy, the reality, is a biological, social and religious treasure to be fostered by those who possess its disposition, whether by nature or grace, for the growth of life on this planet." Gandhi said: "A nation that does not possess such men is poorer for the want."

However, compulsory celibacy, imposed by the Catholic Church on all who want to become priests, is not just a bad thing. It is an evil thing — leading to even greater evils. When the Catholic Church imposes compulsory celibacy on hundreds of thousands of priests worldwide it creates many monstrous situations as priests try to cope. Compulsory celibacy has contributed to, amongst other things, a huge alcoholism problem among priests; priests with serious mental and nervous difficulties; priests abusing drugs, prescribed and illegal; priests abusing power; and of course the phenomenon of the paedophile priest. We must destroy this evil proscription and remove it forever from the Catholic Church.

In the future, I believe, there will be a small number of celibate and virgin Catholic priests, monks and nuns. The majority will be married. We will have married men and married women priests. And all of them will bring their gifts to the altar.

Most of all we must rid the Church of the greatest evil of all — hypocrisy. In so many ways the Pope, the Vatican, the Curia and the hierarchy within the "Clerical Club" are so hypocritical insisting that people live impossible lives when they know that they themselves are not even trying to live them. The bishops and the clergy are the new Scribes and Pharisees, doing what they want themselves but condemning others.

THE CATHOLIC CHURCH IS TWO THINGS. At the spiritual level, it is *the Family of God*. As the family of God it is good, pure and special. That's because God looks after His family. This family consists not only of "card-carrying" members of the Roman Catholic Church; it is made up of all people on the earth, of all faiths and none. In other words, the human race is the catholic church, the family of God. The word "catholic" means universal. I prefer to see myself as a catholic with a small "c". My view of the church is summed up in the creed I wrote for my 1994 book *A Thorn in the Side*, and which is reprinted at the beginning of this book.

However, the Catholic Church is on the other hand a human empire — a two-thousand-year-old human empire. As such it has all the faults and failings of every human empire. As the oldest surviving human empire it has accumulated more evils than all the other lesser human empires. "Power corrupts and absolute power corrupts absolutely" — that's why the Catholic Church is so corrupt. It has exercised absolute power over people and as a result the Catholic Church is, in its human manifestation, absolutely corrupt.

The Catholic Church has perfected the abuse of power, the abuse of money, greed, sexual exploitation, racism, sexism, ageism, homophobia, paedophilia, and every other "ism", "phobia" and "philia" you could conceive of or name. As a system, the human side of the Catholic Church is as rotten and as evil as you'll find!

How can these two aspects — family of God and human empire — exist side by side? I think it is explained by one of Jesus' Gospel parables when he says that the landowner allowed the wheat and the weeds to grow side by side until harvest time. At harvest time the reapers will come and separate the wheat from the weeds. The wheat will be stored in the barns and the weeds burned on a fire. That's what my faith tells me anyway. I am a Catholic in the sense that I am part of the family of God. I have no allegiance or loyalty to the vicious and corrupt human institution that is centred at Rome.

At Rome, the mantra seems to be: "You can mess around with women, men, boys and girls. You can mess around with drink, with drugs and with gambling. You can play around with money and property. But don't touch the power. Leave the power alone." The biggest sin you can commit as a Catholic is to challenge the church's power. They will tolerate all other sins. But not the challenge to power. They are eternally jealous of their absolute power over people.

Paedophile priests will be forgiven by the hierarchy for forty years of child abuse. They will be covered up for. They will be hidden. They will be given money to bribe their victims into silence. They will be received back after prison. They will seldom be laicised, defrocked or excommunicated. When they die they will be given full honours at their funeral. Look at the case of Fr Brendan Smyth in Ireland. His monastery buried him with a Requiem Mass at four in the morning.

But the same church refuses sacraments to sincere Catholic divorced people who are just looking for a second chance at life and love!

Take a priest and a bishop like me: I have committed the greatest sin. I have challenged their power. They rant and they rave. They suspend and they excommunicate. They issue lying press releases. They are consumed with hatred for the man or woman who challenges their absolute power.

During my last interview with Cardinal Cahal Daly in 1985 he asked me, "Do you believe that when I speak God speaks?" I said, "No!" Blood rushing to his face, he demanded: "Have you never read the letters of St Ignatius of Antioch? I have read them and in an original form. Ignatius says: 'The voice of the bishop is the voice of God.'"

Cahal Daly believed that when he spoke God spoke. How more power-crazed can you be than to believe that when you speak God Almighty speaks? The Roman Catholic Church authorities want Catholics to believe that God speaks to the Pope, the Pope speaks to the bishops, the bishops speak to the priests and the priests speak to the people. In this model, the lay people are "the lowest form of church life". The joke among priests is: "Treat the laity like mushrooms. Keep them in the dark and throw plenty of shit on them." But it's not a joke. This is what happens in practice and is desperately cynical and sad.

WHERE DOES MAN'S LUST FOR POWER come from? What is behind his craving for power? The answer is very complex and is found deep in man's psyche, his psychology and his spirituality.

Man's strongest primary instinct is survival and self-preservation. He knows this deep down in his very genes. Like all animals, man the animal sees others as his potential destroyers. Man was born and lives looking over his shoulder. His primal fear is that some creature more powerful than he will conquer him, overpower him, snuff him out. One way to avoid this is to become as powerful as you can become and dominate as many others as you possibly can. The more powerful man feels, the more "security" he feels he has. Those he dominates are no threat to him. They subject themselves to him. They do not attack him. They protect him and hold him in awe. In grasping power, men feel less vulnerable and in dominating others he boosts his self-esteem and his ego.

The desire to have power and control others is at the very centre of man's psyche. Some people achieve their power by becoming kings and queens and prime ministers. Others become popes and bishops and priests. Others become domineering husbands and wives. Others do it by seeking jobs in uniform. All mankind is, to a greater or lesser degree, affected by the fear of powerlessness and annihilation and the consequent need to dominate.

But man also knows that he is fragile, vulnerable and weak. At his very core he feels this vulnerability. Instinctively he knows anxiety, fear, despair. In his body he feels pain and ageing. In his spirit he feels his mortality. So while, on the one hand, man feels he wants power and wants to dominate, on the other he wants to be dominated. He wants someone else to reassure him in the face of insecurity and mortality. Man needs an "other" who is not limited as he is. Erich Fromm in his book *The Fear of Freedom* deals with this tendency to dominate others:

> The first mechanism of escape from freedom . . . is the tendency to give up the independence of one's own individual self and to fuse oneself with somebody or something outside oneself in order to acquire the strength which the individual self is lacking.

IN THE CATHOLIC CHURCH we see all these complex and primal urges of mankind in full play.

In an unthinking recognition of their own ultimate powerlessness, the Catholic hierarchy — the Pope, the bishops and the clergy — submit themselves to God (often a god of their own making or shaping) and submit themselves to the ecclesiastical structures. This offers these clerics the ultimate hedge against powerlessness — falling back on an "other" (God) and a system (Church) which has a guarantee of eternal victory and happiness. That solves their own powerlessness dilemma. But that's not enough. For their sojourn in this life, they need to dominate others so that they feel secure and powerful. And so the Pope and Rome dominate the bishops. The bishops dominate the priests. The priests dominate the lay people.

Everybody co-operates in this conspiracy. The clergy enjoy being on pedestals and the lay people need to put them up on the pedestals so that they will have little mini-gods to look to. In return, everybody is allowed to be members of the club and is promised respectability and belonging in this life and "pie in the sky when they die".

Recently I met a woman who said to me, "Deep down I think like you do. I question things. But are you not afraid? I'd be afraid to go against the Church. I'd be afraid I wouldn't get into heaven." She had been brought up believing that God and the clergy were one and the same thing.

In this set-up God is on high, the ordinary lay people are at the bottom and the clergy and hierarchy are in between, mediating. The clerics have organised things so well in their own interests that they have convinced the lay people that they can only get to God through them and in turn God only speaks to the lay people through the clergy and the hierarchy. Over a two-thousand-year period Catholic popes, bishops and clergy have hijacked God and all the channels of communication to God. They are now the sole suppliers. Men and women can only speak to God through the priests and God will only answer through the priests. If you want the priests to communicate your messages to God and bring you back messages from God you must do what the priests say. You must obey them. You must pay them. You must treat them with awe, deference and respect. When you find out that they are human, and have the same failings as all humans, you must ignore those facts, this nakedness, and admire the emperor's new clothes.

WHERE DOES SEX COME INTO THIS power game? I discussed above how self-preservation is our primary instinct. In the past popes and churchmen used the threat of force as a way of commanding obedience. If you disobeyed the pope, a bishop or an abbot, you could be flogged, thrown in the dungeon or even killed. Things are a bit more civilised today — at least superficially. But the Vatican and Catholic "mafia" are still capable of a sort of violence — psychological and spiritual violence.

After the self-preservation instinct, our next great instinct, and therefore our great vulnerability, is the instinct to reproduce. If you cannot threaten people with torture, the dungeon and death, then the next best thing you can do to control them is to dominate them at the level of their sexuality. The Church has always done that and tries still, with varied success, to do it to this present day.

Human beings have always had a deep hang-up about sexuality, genitalia and the body. I don't believe that this hang-up is instinctual; a bull is not embarrassed if you catch him having sex in a field with a cow; a horse is not embarrassed if you spot his erection; a monkey in a zoo is not embarrassed by his genitalia. But men and women are different. We are embarrassed by our nakedness, our arousal and the exposure of our fantasies and actions. However, I think this embarrassment is a learned embarrassment — learned from our parents, society and the Church, and not necessarily in that order.

Little children often do not have these hang-ups. I remember in the early 1980s visiting a house regularly in Belfast. I used to go for dinner, a drink and an overnight stay. They had a little three-year-old boy. One night after dinner, he came over and stood in front of me. He pulled down his trousers and said, "Father Buckie, tickle my birdie." I was embarrassed and everybody laughed at my blushes. Apparently his mother used to tickle his "birdie" when putting him to bed or giving him a bath. He thought he would like me to do the same! The child's innocence and lack of hang-up was so natural to him.

The hang-up that the rest of us have comes primarily, I think, from religion and the church. We, our parents and our societies only consolidate the hang-up that the Church has imposed on us. That hang-up goes back to the teaching that the body is bad and the spirit good. It is about sex being bad and virginity good. It is about women being bad and men being good. It is about marriage being "tolerable" and celibacy being good.

The Catholic Church, over centuries and generations, has made us all slaves — slaves to guilt, hang-ups and repression. The Church did this through its constant negative teaching and preaching. But it did it best of all when it got us into the confessional. There, priests (with major hang-ups themselves) interrogated us about "bad thoughts, bad actions with ourselves and bad actions with others". They invaded our very souls, destroyed us with condemnations and penances and sent us away from the confessional full of repression and guilt. If you committed a sexual sin you committed a serious "mortal sin". If you didn't tell it in confession you committed a "sacrilege". If you didn't stop doing it they refused you absolution and communion. If you didn't get absolution and communion you went to Hell when you died. All this, an eternity of suffering and unhappiness, because of *sex*!

The Catholic Church has always used sex to control and dominate people. And we, the people, have let them away with it. Now the Church feels that it can tell you when to have and when not to have sex, which sexual acts are permitted and which are not. Most Catholics today have rejected the Catholic Church's teaching on sex altogether, or simply pay it lip-service. They are right to follow their consciences. But a huge legacy of repression and guilt remains. Many people still have to make the journey from sexual slavery to sexual mental health.

The religious leaders of Jesus' day literally crucified the historical Christ. The Catholic Church has crucified people with sexual guilt and sexual repression. Popes, bishops and priests have laid burdens on men's and women's shoulders and have not lifted a finger to help. Condemnation is the order of the day. So many people today feel hurt, abandoned and alienated by the Church and its sexual teachings. In crucifying Christ's brothers and sisters with sexual guilt and repression, the Church is crucifying Christ all over again.

AS THIS BOOK GOES TO PRESS we have buried Pope John Paul II and have just seen the election of the former German Cardinal Joseph Ratzinger as Pope Benedict XVI. The Catholic Church is at a very distinct crossroads.

When John Paul was elected in 1978 I was full of hope for a better, more liberal and more compassionate Church. Here was a young Pope in his fifties from Eastern Europe. He had acted on stage and was a keen sportsman. He had female actress friends. He had fought totalitarianism in the state and was a dedicated enemy of depersonalising communism. I thought that the Italian stranglehold on the Vatican and its curia had finally been broken and that we were in for a new era — no, a new epoch.

I was to be bitterly disappointed. John Paul II, while being an absolute extrovert and the most travelled pope in history, became more and more conservative and reactionary on church teaching, particularly in relation to sexuality. He resisted the move to optional celibacy for the clergy and forbade the world's Catholic bishops even to discuss the topic. He was implacably opposed to the ordination of women. He took the strongest of lines on contraception, even opposing the use of condoms as disease prevention in AIDS-torn Africa. He refused to relax church discipline on divorce and remarriage. He refused to lead the church to a more enlightened dialogue with the homosexual community and during his reign described homosexuality as being "gravely disordered".

Though himself politically up to his neck in Polish and world politics, he reprimanded and sacked priests and theologians in South America for their liberation theology and their active opposition to totalitarian and murderous political regimes. In front of millions he stood over Nicaraguan poet, priest and government minister Ernesto Cardenal, waving the autocratic finger of disapproval and reprimand. The man who had resisted and defeated political totalitarianism in Poland and Eastern Europe had ushered a new level of Inquisition-like totalitarianism into the Catholic Church!

In his latter years, John Paul became the victim of Parkinson's disease and became a shadow of his former self. Some people greatly admired and praised him for his determination to go on. Others, like myself, saw a sick old Pope as symbolic of a sick old Church, especially in Europe. We also felt that Pope John Paul was a sad example of the human temptation to cling to power to the bitter end.

The funeral of John Paul II was not the funeral of the vicar of the utterly powerless Christ. It was the funeral, I thought, of a twenty-first-century Roman Emperor — attended as it was by kings, queens, princes, princesses, presidents and prime ministers. It was undeniably a mighty spectacle. But it was the funeral of a powerful man of this world and personally the words of Christ that echoed in my mind were: "Woe to you when the world speaks well of you. This was the way their fathers treated the false prophets."

For me the real man of God is a man like Archbishop Oscar Romero of San Salvador who was gunned down by his corrupt government while celebrating Mass because he publicly condemned their corruption and publicly challenged their oppression of the poor. John Paul II canonised hundreds of saints but the martyr of El Salvador was not among them. Vatican politics and Vatican international diplomacy and politicking judged Romero unworthy of the martyr's crown. But Romero would have attracted those other words of Christ: "Blessed are you when the world speaks ill of you. This was the way their fathers treated the true prophets."

John Paul II's papacy began in 1978 as a blazing new sunrise but it ended in 2005 as a dark, whimpering sunset giving way, in Europe and the West at least, to a night of doubt and fear.

WHEN CARDINAL JOSEPH RATZINGER walked out on the balcony of St Peter's in Rome as Pope Benedict XVI I was so stunned as to be struck speechless and stuck to my chair! My first thought was: "Where was the Holy Spirit during the conclave?" My second thought was: "Can I even believe in a Holy Spirit any more after this?"

I had watched Cardinal Joseph Ratzinger for twenty years as the head of the Congregation for the Doctrine of the Faith — the modern name for the Inquisition. Ratzinger had published the very conservative Catholic Catechism and many very reactionary documents on sexuality and ecumenism. He had been responsible for investigating liberal theologians and for disciplining and sacking them.

In many respects he was Pope John Paul II's "enforcer" and "tough cop". He had started off life as a reasonably liberal theologian and an open-minded advisor at the Second Vatican Council in the late 1950s and early 1960s. But during the late 1960s and as a result of student unrest in Germany, Ratzinger became afraid of the liberal way and quickly and increasingly became conservative and right-wing.

We had all more or less accepted that there would be no change during John Paul II's time — especially with Ratzinger at the doctrine congregation. With John Paul's death many of us hoped that there might be a new pope, from the developing world perhaps, a pope who would put internal church renewal close to the top of his priorities with other important issues like international human rights. Names of cardinals from Africa and South America were mentioned. There was, once again, the beginnings of an air of hope and optimism in the Church.

That the cardinals should meet in conclave and very quickly elect Joseph Ratzinger was indescribably shocking.

We are at the very beginning of the papacy of Benedict XVI. I am writing these words literally only days into that papacy. I believe that either of two things will happen: Benedict XVI will continue as Cardinal Ratzinger did, enunciating the most conservative of Catholic doctrines and laws and enforcing them with a harsh discipline; or else Pope Benedict will have a complete conversion, throw off the enforcer mantle and adopt the mantle of a listening, compassionate spiritual father. He could appoint some other churchman to his old job at the doctrine congregation who could then be the new tough cop and enforcer and allow Benedict to spend the last phase of his life in the new role of compassionate, listening, spiritual father.

As of now, I do not know which way it will go. So I have decided to give Benedict XVI the benefit of the doubt and wait and see. As the Lord says: "It is by their fruits that ye shall know them." I, like many others, am waiting to see whether or not the German Shepherd is capable of becoming the Good Shepherd!

Chapter Nine

JESUS, SEXUALITY AND LOVE

"I see in Jesus a compelling picture of male sexual wholeness, of creative masculinity, and of the redemption of manhood from both oppressiveness and superficiality" — James Nelson, US Theologian

TWICE IN THE ONE YEAR recently I was asked to give a talk in two Irish universities on the topic *Was Jesus Gay?* I didn't at all mind addressing this question, even though it is certainly controversial and provocative. But there is no question that cannot be asked and there is no answer that we should ever shy away from giving.

Some fundamentalist Christians would regard a discussion on Jesus' sexuality and sexual life as blasphemous. They are wrong. If we ever allowed these people to stifle our freedom we would become prisoners of silence, the Christian equivalent of Salman Rushdie.

WAS JESUS GAY? The truthful answer is that we do not know what Jesus' sexual orientation was. I think that it is good that we do not know because it does not really matter. What matters is that Jesus — unlike his present-day Church — has no problem accepting and loving all his brothers and sisters as they are, regardless of their sexual orientation. The Pope does not speak for Christ when he says that homosexuality is disordered, that it is always a sin and that discrimination against homosexuals can be sometimes justified. This type of pronouncement from the Pope is an evil pronouncement and feeds discrimination against the homosexual community.

If we want to discover the kind of man Jesus was, we need to look at the best biography we have of him — the New Testament. Jesus was a very whole person, an integrated person. He was in touch with his feelings, his needs, his humanity. As such Jesus, like all mature and whole people, had integrated his sexuality and his spirituality.

If I was looking for a modern insight into the humanity of Christ, I would look no further than Martin Scorsese's great film *The Last Temptation of Christ*. It is the very best exploration I have seen of Christ's humanity.

JESUS WAS ON CLOSE AND INTIMATE TERMS with women in general but particularly with several individual women in the Gospels. He had a great bond with his mother Mary. He did not leave home until he was thirty and even then his mother went with him. We have very little information on the hidden life of Christ at Nazareth between the ages of twelve and thirty. But we know he felt a sense of independence. At the age of twelve, he felt free enough to disappear from his parents in Jerusalem and remain missing for several days. He was not at all apologetic when his exasperated parents, Mary and Joseph, found him in the Temple! So while Jesus was close to Mary he was also independent. If Mary was tempted to be a dominant mother, Christ resisted. In the Temple he told her: "I must be about my Father's business." Mary accompanied her son for his three-year ministry. She persuaded him to perform his first miracle at the wedding feast at Cana. She was with him during his darkest hours on the cross.

Christ had a very special relationship with Mary Magdala. Legend says that she was a prostitute, but there is no evidence for that. The Gospels do make it patently clear that she was possessed by seven demons — not just one, seven! She was a troubled woman when she met Christ. He changed her life completely. There were obviously the deepest, the most intense emotions between Jesus and Mary Magdala.

When Jesus rose from the dead and wanted a first witness to the resurrection, he did not choose his "sinless" mother Mary to be that witness. Nor did he choose St John, "the disciple Jesus loved". Nor did Jesus choose Peter, the first pope, or any of the other apostles. He chose Mary of Magdala. Mary was in the garden at the empty tomb. She saw Jesus but didn't recognise him. Supposing him to be the gardener, she asked for Jesus. As soon as He said "Mary" she knew Him. She cried out "Rabbuni!" and was about to embrace Him when He said: "Do not grasp me, for I have not yet ascended to my Father and your Father." But it was interesting that her first instinctive reaction was to embrace Him. This suggests to me that they were in the habit of physically embracing each other, that they had a physical relationship. When Jesus asked Mary not to grasp Him until after He had ascended, by implication He was saying that it had been alright to grasp Him in the past and it would be alright to do so in the future.

Mary Magdala is my favourite saint. I mention her name at every Mass I say. When I think of her I think of the great sinner that became a great saint. I also think that if Mary Magdala could be used by God and make it to heaven, then so can I. For me, Mary Magdala is a lighthouse of hope. When I think of her, I also think of two wise sayings: "Every saint has a past and every sinner has a future"; and "A saint is just a sinner who kept trying".

In his book *Spiritual Sex*, Nik Douglas says of Mary Magdala:

> Followers of some Gnostic sects believed that Jesus had an erotic relationship with Mary Magdalene, to whom he gave secret teachings. It's very likely that Jesus and Mary Magdalene were married. Nowhere in the Bible does it say that Jesus was not married, or that he was celibate. As a Jew and a Rabbi, for Jesus to be recognised as a spiritual teacher, he had to be married . . .

> The Gnostic Gospel of Philip states that Jesus "used to kiss Mary often on the mouth". The Gospel of Mary, another lost text rediscovered in 1896, suggests that Mary Magdala, a former prostitute, was a visionary and spiritual teacher whose insights surpassed those of the Apostles. Other Gnostic texts suggest that Mary Magdalene was the leader of a group of twelve female apostles and that she had extraordinary occult powers.

In another fascinating book, *Bloodline of the Holy Grail: The Hidden Lineage of Jesus Revealed*, the author Laurence Gardner insists that Jesus and Mary Magdala were indeed husband and wife. He says:

> Early Christian texts describe Mary Magdalene as "the woman who knew the all". She was the one whom "Christ loved more than all the disciples"; she was "the apostle endowed with knowledge, vision and insight, far exceeding Peter's"; and she was the beloved bride who anointed Jesus at the Sacred Marriage (*Hieros Gamos*) at Bethany.

Gardner goes on to discuss the plot of the Roman Church to downplay Mary Magdalene's role as Jesus' wife:

> The Roman Church elected to discredit Mary Magdalene in an attempt to exalt her mother-in-law, Jesus' mother Mary. In order to accomplish this, they made use of ambiguous comments in the New Testament — comments that described the unmarried Magdalene as a "sinner" (which actually meant she was a celibate almah undergoing assessment in betrothal). The duplicitous bishops decided however, that a sinful woman must be a whore and Mary was branded as such thereafter.

Gardner continues and suggests to us the reason for the plot to downgrade Mary and her relationship/marriage with Christ:

> Mary's legacy remained the greatest of all threats to a fearful Church that had bypassed Messianic descent in favour of a self-styled Apostolic Succession.

Gardner's book is a worthwhile, riveting read.

Do I think that Jesus and Mary Magdala were husband and wife? The honest answer is that I don't know but I think that it is perfectly possible. Their descendants could very well be alive today. If I found it to be true, it would enhance my faith rather than damage it or challenge it.

But I could see how such a thought would shake popes, curia and Church hierarchy! Then that's exactly what Jesus did, was it not? I do know that the Church we have today is not the kind of Church that Christ founded. One of the reformers has said: "What Christ preached was a kingdom; what we got was a Church." I agree. I do know that from earliest times real truths have been hidden by churchmen and false truths have been promulgated. I take Gardner's point about messianic descent versus apostolic succession very seriously. Our Catholic Church is based, in large part, on empire-building, patriarchy, the subjugation of women, power, mind control and a dozen other negative and soul-destroying forces.

JESUS WAS ALSO ON INTIMATE TERMS with two other female friends — Martha and Mary, who lived in Bethany and who were the sisters of Jesus' great male friend Lazarus. But His relationship with the two women was very different.

Martha was the practical one — the cook, the baker, the waitress and the homemaker. When we meet them in the Gospel Jesus has come to their house for a break, to rest and to get away from the crowds. Martha ministers to Jesus through her home-making. He felt safe and looked after in Martha's house. He may have gently reprimanded her with the words: "Martha, Martha, you worry and fret about so many things. But only one thing is necessary." Jesus loved Martha. The Gospels say so. He loved her especially because she ministered to him. Martha was Jesus' retreat, His bolt-hole, His refuge from the storm. Martha was another of the women Jesus loved.

And her sister Mary? Jesus had a very different relationship with Mary — but a close and intimate relationship. Mary sat at Jesus' feet and chatted with him. One only sits at the feet of someone to whom one is devoted, such as a lover or a parent. Mary was most comfortable at Jesus' feet; and Jesus loved having her there. Jesus on the divan and Mary at His feet — this was a posture of great trust and intimacy. Of what did they speak? I think we must only believe that they opened up their hearts to each other. In fact, they spoke of things so important that Jesus said of Mary: "Mary has chosen the better part."

OTHER WOMEN ARE MENTIONED in the Gospels who shared some intimacy with Jesus. Jesus was at a feast in one of the Pharisee's houses. After dinner a "sinful" woman came in (maybe Mary Magdala). She knelt down and washed Jesus' feet with her tears, dried them with her hair and then anointed them. The Pharisees were enraged that a sinful woman was allowed to get away with this action. Jesus stood up for her. He said: "Her great love has cancelled out her many sins." He also said: "Wherever the gospel is read this deed of hers will be remembered to her." Washing someone's feet with your tears and drying them with your hair is an act of great sensuality and intimacy. Both Jesus and the woman were perfectly at ease with this sensuality and intimacy.

Jesus formed an instant relationship and friendship with another woman — the Samaritan woman at the well. They talked at length. He asked her for water and then He gave her the water of faith. He, a Jew, was not supposed to talk to a Samaritan woman. But He broke that convention too and spoke to her and befriended her and gave her faith.

Jesus stood up for another woman in front of the Scribes and the Pharisees — the woman caught in the act of adultery. The crowd was about to stone her and they asked Jesus to agree with them. We are told that Jesus bent down and wrote something on the sand. Legend says that He wrote down the sins of all of those standing around condemning the woman. Then He said: "Let him who is without sin cast the first stone." They all dropped their stones and walked away with red faces. Jesus had reminded them that they were all sinners, all hypocrites. Then He looked at the woman with love and said: "Has no one condemned you? Neither do I condemn you. Go and sin no more."

And what of Jesus' marvellous encounter with Veronica during the last hours of His life? He was struggling under His cross to Calvary, weak, His face covered with blood and sweat. I'm sure that he could not even see as the blood and sweat blinded Him. The hostile crowd was cheering and jeering. He was totally alone. Who would dare defy the Romans and chief priests and go to his help?

A woman did. She was called Veronica. She braved the jeering, cynical crowd and got her towel and walked out to Jesus and wiped His suffering face. We can only imagine the love that impelled Veronica to risk death to act as she did. We can only imagine how Jesus loved her for what she did. Christ's love for her was so palpable that legend tells us that a miracle occurred. The countenance of Jesus' face was imprinted upon Veronica's towel — the only picture of the Saviour — painted by the Divine Artist Himself and not in oils or watercolours but in His Precious Blood. Did Jesus not love Veronica? Did Veronica not love Jesus?

WHAT OF MEN? Jesus had intimate relationships with men. The Gospels prove this beyond any doubt.

Lazarus was the brother of Martha and Mary. St John tells us that "Jesus loved Martha and her sister Mary and their brother Lazarus". When Lazarus was sick and dying the sisters sent the following message to Jesus: "Lord, the man you love is ill." When Jesus arrived at Bethany and found that Lazarus was dead and had been buried for four days, He asked to be taken to the grave. He wept so bitterly that all the Jews who had come to sympathise with Martha and Mary said: "See how much he loved him." There is nothing to argue about. From the words of Christ Himself in the Bible we see that Jesus had a deep, intimate and emotional relationship with Lazarus.

In the Gospel of John the apostle John describes himself as "the beloved disciple" and as "the disciple that Jesus loved". John did not just mean the same love as Jesus had for all the disciples. He goes out of his way to show that the love that he and Jesus shared was a deeper love than He had for the other disciples. And we don't just rely on words. At the Last Supper Jesus lay on the divan with John's head on His breast. No one can deny that this was an act of great intimacy and closeness. Were two men to lie like this today at a function, people would be at least thinking, "Are those two men gay?" Jesus and John shared a wonderful intimacy.

Jesus was approached on His journeys by a rich young man who wanted to be one of his disciples. Jesus told the young man to sell all he owned and follow Him. The young man couldn't do this as he was a man of great wealth. Jesus allowed him to walk away sad. But at the beginning of this story, the Gospels say of Jesus: "He looked at him and loved him." Jesus saw something very special in that young man, something that He loved, something that He found attractive enough to feel that He loved him.

Jesus greatly needed the love and affection of His male disciples and friends. One night at supper Jesus said three times to Peter: "Simon Peter, do you love me more than these others do?" Jesus had the same need in the Garden of Gethsemane on Holy Thursday evening. He was a man who constantly needed love, affection and companionship from His male friends and disciples.

I AM SURE THAT SOME WILL REGARD the question: "Was Jesus straight, gay or bisexual?" as blasphemous. But it is not. As Christians, we believe that Jesus was one hundred per cent human as well as one hundred per cent divine. If He was one hundred per cent human that means that His body was exactly like the body of every other man who lived before Him or who has lived since. That means that Jesus had genitalia — a penis and two testicles. There is no reason to believe that He was any kind of eunuch.

If Jesus was one hundred per cent human, that also means that He had a sex drive, that He experienced sexual arousal and that His body needed, regularly, to discharge semen. Again, the only way not to believe this is to believe that Jesus was sexually dysfunctional! Why should we even want to think that?

The central question here then is: "Was Jesus sexually active? Did He ever have sex?" Sex and sexuality are good gifts from God. They only become "bad" or "immoral" when we use those gifts to hurt, use or abuse. I believe that Jesus was God and incapable of sin. So I know that He never deliberately hurt, used or abused anyone. So I believe that Jesus never committed a sexual sin.

But I do believe that Jesus was sexually active and that, in the context of love, He experienced sexual intimacy. "He was like us in all things but sin." I do not know if Jesus had sex with anyone. If He did I do not know whether it was with a man or a woman. And I know that if it happened it was "making love" and not just sex.

Did Jesus masturbate and have "wet dreams". Of course He did. He was a normal man. But the answer to the question "Was Jesus gay?" is that we simply do not know, and I think this is a good thing. All we need to know is that Jesus was the Greatest Lover of All Time! And He loves and blesses us when we use our sexuality to make love and He asks us never to use it to hurt, use or abuse.

Chapter Ten

A NEW SPIRITUALITY OF SEX

*"Passion between the covers of a book
May come in the form of the undraped body of
Anybody's whore.
Or the naked form of
A man hanging from a
Cross-armed tree
Disarmingly unarmed,
Save for the look of love"*
— Sherwood A. Treadwell, The Christian Century

THE CATHOLIC CHURCH MESSED UP my head (and every other head) when it came to sex. They taught me that my body and sex were dirty and that they would both bring me to hell. They told me that my soul was good and that it was the spiritual part of me that would survive if I kept my body under control. While they were preaching this to me and you, cardinals, bishops and priests were active on the gay scene, priests were sexually abusing little children in sacristies and schools, monks were abusing novices in monasteries, Christian Brothers were fondling boys' genitals behind desks in classrooms and nuns, when they were not having sex with priests and each other, were doing God knows what to innocent little children in orphanages and homes.

Just a few days before I wrote this, a young priest, just twelve years ordained and on a leave of absence, rang me and said, "I can no longer work in a Church that I now believe to be intrinsically evil."

That priest is right. The Roman Catholic Church is intrinsically evil; and the twisted and perverse idea of sex that they preach is at the heart of that intrinsic evil.

Of course, I know that there were and are many good and saintly popes, bishops, priests, monks and nuns in the life of the Church. But generally speaking these good ones were given a very bad time by the others and they generally had to suffer greatly for their difference and their goodness.

AT THE RISK OF REPEATING MYSELF, I must say again — in fact, I would like to scream it from the very mountaintops — that our human body is good and one of God's very finest creations. Every part of the body is good, including our genitals. In fact, our genitals are especially good: they are the body parts that God gave us to help Him in His work of creation. Through these parts we "pro-create".

Christianity in general and Catholicism in particular has been dogged by that heresy of dualism that says that the body is bad and the soul is good. More positive people in church history taught that the body was the "Temple of the Holy Spirit". But even this was taught in a way that made us feel we had to keep the body good and holy — in other words, remain celibate — so that the Holy Spirit might come into us and stay with us.

The body is a wonderful creation. Just think of what it is — the brain, the heart, the organs, the muscles, the blood vessels, the skin. What a complex and wonderful creation. Instead of thinking that the body is bad, we should always think of how wonderfully holy and good a creation it is.

The great modern spiritual writer Fr Henri Nouwen lived in great pain. He was gay but could never admit so publicly. Perhaps had he lived a little longer, he might have felt able to "come out"? In his book *The Inner Voice of Love* he wrote a piece entitled "Bring Your Body Home":

A New Spirituality of Sex

You have never felt completely safe in your body. But God wants to love you in all that you are, spirit and body. Increasingly, you have come to see your body as an enemy that has to be conquered. But God wants you to befriend your body so that it can be made ready for the Resurrection. When you do not fully own your body, you cannot claim it for an everlasting life.

How then do you bring your body home? By letting it participate in your deepest desire to receive and offer love. Your body needs to be held and to hold, to be touched and to touch. None of these needs is to be despised, denied or repressed. But you have to keep searching for your body's deeper need, the need for genuine love. Every time you are able to go beyond the body's superficial desires for love, you are bringing your body home and moving towards integration and unity.

In Jesus, God took on human flesh. The Spirit of God overshadowed Mary, and in her all enmity between spirit and body was overcome. Thus God's spirit was united with the human spirit, and the human body became the temple destined to be lifted up into the intimacy of God through the Resurrection. Every human body has been given a new hope, of belonging eternally to the God who created it. Thanks to the Incarnation, you can bring your body home.

IN SOME MONASTERIES AND CONVENTS monks and nuns used to strip to the waist and beat themselves with whips made of leather and cord until they bled. They saw this as bringing the body under control and as penance. Some members of the right-wing Catholic religious organisation Opus Dei still use the whip on themselves! Other monks and nuns used to wear vests made of rough horsehair or even wire to make their bodies do penance. When Cardinal Rafael Merry Del Val of the Vatican died in the early part of the twentieth century they discovered several metal hair shirts in his rooms covered with his congealed blood. Lay people often starved themselves of food and water and some people went regularly to St Patrick's Purgatory at Lough Derg, the island of penance in Ireland, and walked on the sharp stones there until their feet were bruised and bleeding.

This distorted "spirituality" was about punishing the bad, dirty, evil body. Of course, our bodies can be used for sin and badness. We can use our hands to pull a trigger and wield a knife and murder and kill. We can use our tongues to backbite and gossip and cause great emotional suffering. We can stuff ourselves with food and give way to gluttony and bad health. We can abuse our bodies with alcohol, drugs and tobacco. We can use our sexuality to abuse, to assault, to rape and do terrible damage.

But all of these things do not show that the body is bad. They show that the abuse of the body, by us, is bad. But the body itself is good. I want to offer you four "proofs" of the goodness of the body:

1. When God came into the world he could have come as pure spirit or in some sort of "alien" form. But he came in an ordinary human body. God could not have taken on a human body if the human body is a bad thing.

2. The Bible tells us that the body is good. In fact it tells us that the body is the Temple of the Holy Spirit. The Holy Spirit would never reside in anything bad.

3. The body can be used for good. If you had no hands, how could you give to the poor? If you had no feet, how could you visit the sick and the imprisoned? If you had no tongue, how could you offer loud praise to God? If you had no knees or spine, how could you physically reverence God? If you had no heart, how could you love? If you had no genitals, how could you pro-create?

4. Our Christian creed tells us that the body, as well as the soul, will rise again on the Last Day. So our bodies will be in Heaven for eternity. How could anything bad be in Heaven?

So I think it is time we stopped doing our bodies down. It is time we stopped being ashamed of them. It is time we thanked God for the gift of our bodies, as an anonymous writer did in this prayer:

Prayer of Thanks for our Bodies

Thank you for the body that loves me.

My own body;
It tingles with pleasure
And sends me pain as a warning;
It takes in food and air
And transforms them to life;
It reaches orgasmic bliss
And reveals depths of peace.

Thank you for the body that loves me.

My lover's body;
It surrounds me with safe arms,
And senses my needs and joys;
It allows me vulnerability,
And enables my ecstasy;
It teaches me how to love
And touches me with love.

Thank you for the body that loves me.

My spiritual community's body;
It embodies your presence
By empowering prophets,
It inspires me with stories
And enchants me with mystery.

Thank you for the body that loves me.

The cosmic and mystical body;
It calls me to communion
With creatures and creation;
It manifests your glory
And mine as its child;
It upholds my feet
And heals my body.

Thank you for the body that loves me.

What a wonderful prayer: body-positive, in love with creation! I keep it in my breviary and use it all the time as an antidote to the poison of body-hating with which I was infected by false Church teaching.

No one likes lying awake, unable to sleep, at three or four in the morning. But I am so very grateful to have had one sleepless night during 2001. It was on that night that I turned on the BBC World Service and discovered Hafiz — the great Persian poet and prophet of love and wine. Today I am the proud owner of many of Hafiz's works. Hafiz and I are now inseparable friends and always will be.

Hafiz or Shams-ud-din Muhammad Hafiz was born in Isfahan, Persia (Iran) circa 1320 and died in 1389. He is little known in the Western World but he is the most beloved poet in Iran. Hafiz's father died when he was just a child and the family were left in poor circumstances. Hafiz had to work early to help support the family. Until he found patronage for his poetry he worked as a baker and a copyist.

Hafiz educated himself and had one or two very influential teachers. He was very attracted to a beautiful young woman who lived on his bakery round. One day the angel of the Lord appeared to him and Hafiz said: "Angel, you are much more beautiful than the young lady I admire. And if you are so beautiful how much more beautiful God must be. I want God!"

Roger Montgomery introduces Hafiz thus:

> Hafiz was a seeker of wisdom who became a poet of genius, a lover of truth who has transcended the ages. His timeless message of liberation invites us to meet him in the tavern of the human spirit, to share a cup of wine and to enjoy the blissful vision of humanity's highest potential. He emphasises the "enjoy" part. . . . Hafiz, the poet, was a synthesizer of knowledge, a thinker about the human condition, and a reporter on his own journeys into higher awareness. . . . He was a poet of God. . . . Hafiz wrote of the wine of the spirit and the wine of the grape. . . . Such is Hafiz — heart open, intellect detached and soaring, tongue in cheek, a lover of humanity. An incomparable weaver of the mystic and the hedonistic.

Hafiz writes beautifully about the body and about love (taken from *The Subject Tonight Is Love*, edited by Daniel Ladinsky):

I Want You To Have This

I
Want you to have this,
All the beauty in
My
Eyes,

All the
Beauty
Of my mouth,

All the splendour of
My strength,

All the wonder of the
Musk parts of
My body,

For are we not talking
About real
Love.

SEX IS GOOD and one of God's greatest gifts. We can ask why God gave us sex and we can answer that He gave us sex so that children might be brought into the world and so that men and women might experience ecstasy and pleasure with each other. And that is fine. But the very fact that God thought of creating sex and did create sex means that it is a good in itself and *not just* because it enables humans to have babies or experience pleasure.

As I hope I have demonstrated in the first part of this book, for the early part of my life I believed the lie that sex was bad. I nearly drove myself mad running to confession with my "impure thoughts" and "impure actions" with myself. I thought that these things were "mortal sins" that would cut me off from God and bring me to Hell. I went through mental torture right until I was in my thirties and forties.

Then, nervously and hesitatingly, I discovered sexual expression with others in the context of friendship, tenderness and love. And I found sex wonderful, holy and freeing.

I agree with St Augustine when he said that our hearts were made for God and that we would never find rest until we found rest in Him. But I have really come to know that when we can bond spiritually, mentally and physically with another human being, we experience something of the wonderful pleasure of that perfect and eternal bonding we will have with God when we go to Him.

I know that when I have enjoyed sex with someone who was warm and caring and intimate and loving, I have leapt across that great gulf of separation that we humans feel, and that I felt very whole, very calm and very centred. I see sex as a sacrament — a sacrament of the ultimate bonding that I will have with God in eternity and in Heaven. In that sense, then, sexuality does not separate us from God or make us forget Him — unless we take the wrong approach to it. In fact, sexuality and sex, properly used and properly integrated into one's life, lead one to God, can put one in touch with God. I believe that sex can be and is prayer and worship.

In the past "they" told me that abstinence from sex leads one to God. A small minority of people in the world and in the church are called to find and embrace God through celibacy and sexual abstinence. But the majority of us are called to find God through the embracing of the self, the body and sexuality. They are just two different but equally authentic ways to the same God.

I LOVE THOSE WORDS from the Anglican Marriage Rite where the couple says to each other: "With my body I thee worship." Each partner is offering their body to be at the other's service for life. I know that this does not just mean sexually. They are also saying, "By the labour of my body and the sweat of my brow I will love you" or "By my daily labour in our home I will love you."

But there is a real sense in which men and women, in marriage, use their bodies to worship each other. Lovers often say to each other, "I love you. I worship you. I worship the ground on which you walk." And this is fitting especially in married love and in Christian marriage. We Christians (some of us at least) believe that marriage is a sacrament. Marriage is traditionally seen as a sacrament of God and His love for His bride, the Church. So when husbands and wives make love, not only are they rightfully loving and worshipping each other, they are actually worshipping God. "With my body I thee worship."

If we say a morning offering and offer all our thoughts, words, sufferings and actions to God, then we make everything in our day holy. When we wash, we give praise to God. When we work, we praise. When we cook, clean and eat, we worship. And when we make love, we are offering God a prayer and an act of worship. "With my body I thee worship." Of course, this is not true of sex that hurts, abuses or uses. That would be a contradiction.

Down through the ages, holy men and women — the mystics — have talked about prayer and meditation as making love to God and God making love to us. For them, sexuality and spirituality are very closely aligned. Below, I quote just a few of them.

The Christian Hilary of Poitiers said: "By means of my flesh I was drawing near to God, by means of my faith I was called to new birth. . . . I was assured that I could not be reduced to non-being."

Maximus the Confessor wrote:

> God is the producer and generator of tenderness and Eros. He has set outside himself what was in himself, namely, creatures. Which is why it is said of him: "God is love." *The Song of Songs* calls him *agape*, or sensual "pleasure", and "desire", which means Eros. In so far as the Eros desire originates from him, he can be said to be the moving force of it, since he generated it. But in so far as he himself is the true object of the love, he is the moving force in others who look to him and possess according to their own nature the capacity for desire.

John Climacus said: "Blessed is the person whose desire for God has become like the lover's passion for the beloved."

Julian of Norwich wrote:

> God is the means whereby our Substance and our Sensuality are kept together so as never to be apart. . . . Both our Substance and our Sensuality together may rightfully be called our Soul. That is because they are both oned in God. Our Sensuality is the beautiful City in which Our Lord Jesus sits and in which He is enclosed.

The Christian Bible is full of references to God as lover. *The Song of Songs* is about God as lover. And in the Prophet Hosea we see Israel referred to as the bride of God who has gone away and been unfaithful to him but whom he is prepared to take back.

It was D.H. Lawrence who said: "When sensuality and spirituality combine they become an unstoppable force."

And, finally, my friend Hafiz wants God's kisses and says God wants kisses and "sweet threatening shouts":

You Better Start Kissing Me

Throw away
All your begging bowls at God's door,

For I have heard the Beloved
Prefers sweet threatening shouts,

Something on the order of:

"Hey, Beloved,
My heart is a raging volcano
Of love for you!

You better start kissing me —
Or Else!"

(From *I Heard God Laughing*, edited by David Ladinsky)

I WAS ALSO TAUGHT that when I died and went to Heaven I would receive the "Beatific Vision". In other words I would be risen, saved and glorified and would be able to see God and tolerate that sight. The Bible had told me that "No man can see God and live", but in Heaven, by God's grace, I can look upon God and not die. This Beatific Vision would go on for all eternity and I would be so hypnotised and enthralled by it I would simply be lost in love and worship eternally. My mind can just about grasp the proposed image.

But then I asked myself, what is there on earth, in my human life, that is something of a foretaste, a sacrament of that eternal enthralment? Everything in Heaven has a dim reflection of it on the earth.

A New Spirituality of Sex

I can remember reading in a spiritual book some years ago of how we meet God in the "O God" moments of our lives. We go to the top of a mountain and are overcome by the beauty of the scene below and we exclaim: "O God!" That's a pleasurable "O God" moment. Or we just hear that someone we love has died and we drop into a chair and put our head in our hands and say: "O God." That's an anguished and suffering "O God" moment. It is as if we meet God best in the "O God" moments — the moments of agony and ecstasy — and not the mundane moments of life. Jesus was talking about something related to this experience when he said: "Would that you were cold or hot. But you are lukewarm and I will spit you out of my mouth." We don't meet God in the lukewarm. We meet him in the hot and the cold.

I know that we meet God in life's sufferings and anguish. Olivier Clement in his wonderful book *The Roots of Christian Mysticism* addresses the issue of how anguish and sufferings brings us to God:

> But our very anguish is a source of grace, for it betrays a longing for being and unity, a yearning to know the Being and the One. . . . Through anguish and wonder humanity has some inkling of the great depth of divine wisdom.

The opposite is equally true. We also meet God in the "O God" moments of ecstasy. We find God in a beautiful symphony, in Handel's *Messiah*, in a poem, in a song, in nature. The list is endless really.

But what of the sexual orgasm? Is that not one of the most pleasurable and ecstatic "O God" moments of all? Do not lovers cry out, as they make love, and as they are about to climax and reach orgasm: "O God, O God, O God"? How can you tell me that God is not in those "O God" moments? Of course he is. In fact he is there especially. For through sex and the making of love, men and women are touching the Creator. The Creator's hair is glancing off their skins, full of the goose-pimples of pleasure. It is no accident, believe me, that men and women scream out "O God" as they are about to climax and orgasm.

And so sexual orgasm is a sacrament of the Beatific Vision. It is a small share in this world of the orgasmic pleasure that we are to experience in the next world. "Eye has not seen; nor has ear heard; nor has it entered into the heart of man; the wonderful things that God has prepared for those who love him." I know that on occasions when I experienced a very pleasurable orgasm I felt a wild sense both of abandon and of centredness that I have never felt in any other way.

People jokingly ask the old clichéd question after love-making: "Did the earth move for you?" How wonderful it is when a couple can say that the earth moved for them both. How much more wonderful it is when we come to believe and know that God is intimately involved in our sexual earth-moving experiences and that he regards them not as sins done in darkness but as acts of worship and prayer. And how wonderful it is to realise that when we meet God the earth will move so much and so completely that we will be translated to Eternal Ecstasy: "This day you will be with me in Paradise."

Christ is our greatest lover. Down through the ages, mystics have, in various ways, thought, written and prayed about Christ as lover. This is a most authentic approach. I have had occasional "erotic" moments with Christ in prayer. They were in their own way "orgasmic". By this I mean the power of the prayer released in me a mystical insight. I had one such moment on 4 July 2000 in the chapel of the Cistercian Monastery at Portglenone, Northern Ireland, when the following prayer came to me:

Sexuality, Sensuality and the Body of Christ
(Before the Blessed Sacrament)

God is Love — John.
Love is God.
All true love is worship.
Love is the opposite of using and abusing.
Loneliness is the search for love.
What's done in loneliness and in search is love trying to find its way.
God made both the body and the soul.
Both are equally good and will live forever.
The negative rejection of the body is a rejection of God.
Only the few have the gift of celibacy.
For most people "It is not good for man to be alone" — Genesis.
There are two paths to God —

A New Spirituality of Sex

For the chosen few there is the way of celibacy and single chastity.
For the chosen many there is the way of loving intimacy with another human being.
One way "abandons" sexual activity to "embrace" God.
The other "embraces" sexual activity and intimacy to "embrace" God.

In another's body we can truly find the Body of Christ.

Christ's beautiful hair.
Christ's sensual skin.
Christ's loving eyes.
Christ's searing tears.
Christ's dimpled cheeks.
Christ's soft lips.
Christ's strong shoulders.
Christ's manly breast.
Christ's thumping heart.
Christ's supporting arms.
Christ's helping hands.
Christ's challenging fists.
Christ's heaving ribs.
Christ's telling scar.
Christ's warm torso.
Christ's granite hips.
Christ's sculptured abdomen.
Christ's cosmic manhood.
Christ's pillar-like legs.
Christ's well-worn knees.
Christ's firm feet.
Christ's punishing heel.

The Eucharist, the Bread and the Wine, is truly the Body of Christ.
But my Brother, my Sister, are also truly the Body of Christ.
My beautiful brothers and sisters are truly the Body of Christ.
My ugly brothers and sisters are truly the Body of Christ.
If I cannot find Christ in others I will *never* find him in the Bread and the Wine.
If I cannot find Christ in my body I will never find him in my soul.
If I cannot find Christ in my sexuality I will never find him in my celibacy.

The Christ of my agonies must also be the Christ of my ecstasies and orgasms.

It is at "Oh God" moments that I find Christ!

O God — that's beautiful!
O God — that's hideous!
O God — what pleasure!
O God — what pain!
O God — how touching!
O God — how sad!
O God — what companionship!
O God — what loneliness!
O God — what a baby!
O God — what a corpse!
O God — what beauty!
O God — what ugliness!
O God — how sweet!
O God — how bitter!
O God! O God.

I believe — no I know — that God gave me these words as an inspiration. Let us all cry out every day we live: "O God! With my body I thee worship!"

ONE OF THE WORST INJUSTICES perpetrated in the history of the human race was the notion that men were good and women were bad and that man was superior to women. This notion has held particular sway in the Catholic Church, where even until today women are not allowed to be ordained. One of the Church Fathers went as far as to say: "The vagina is the gateway to Hell!"

Any authentic spirituality must acknowledge and celebrate the fact that woman is as good as and equal to man. Men and women are different but equal. In the Christian Church especially they should be treated as equal in every respect. They should, for instance, be allowed to be ordained to the three branches of Holy Orders — deacon, priest and bishop.

And let us stop this patronising notion that men are other Jesuses and women are other Virgin Marys — that men should exercise control and power and women should be passive and serve. The great injustices have been done to women throughout history must be stopped. Janet Crawford and Eric Webb have written beautifully of this issue in their *A Litany for Many Voices*, which speaks in the varied voices of the women in the bible, of which I quote just one verse below:

> I am Mary.
> I loved my baby
> For which eternally I must wear
> The patriarchal crown.
> I beseech you, my sisters,
> Help me remove the weight
> And lay it down.

All of us, men and women, who want to travel the spiritual path must help Mary and all women to remove their crown — a crown of thorns — their ancient pain of being denied, isolated and degraded.

THE ISSUE OF WOMEN BECOMING PRIESTS has been a losing battle for the Catholic Church for many years now, and it will not easily be kept off the agenda. In my homily at Mother Frances's ordination, which I discuss later in the book, I pointed out that there is a long history of women being ordained.

- The Precedent of the Virgin Mary: A priest's primary function is to celebrate the Eucharist and to share the Body of Christ. The very first person to give the Body of Christ to the world was the Virgin Mary. If a woman can give Christ to the world physically and literally, as Mary did, then she can certainly give Christ sacramentally.

- When one is ordained *it is the soul that is ordained, not the body*. Gender is irrelevant to ordination.

- The sinful woman who anointed Jesus' feet before his crucifixion (to the scandal of the Pharisees and Patriarchs) received praise from Christ. He said: "What she has done is a good thing. It will be remembered to her wherever the story is told." In a very real sense, Christ was anointed near the end of his life by a woman. That woman was a minister, a priest to Christ.

- Early Christian documents show that Mary and the female disciples were present at the Last Supper — the First Mass — as active participants.

- St Paul writes of Phoebe, a deaconess of the church at Caesarea, and other women engaged in ministry. The Diaconate is a part of Holy Orders.

- St Cyprian writes of a female priest who was an elder of the church at Cappadocia.

- St Priscilla is written of as "the priest officiating along with the other priests in the central act of worship in the church (the Eucharist)".

- In Rome we find, in the catacombs, an icon depicting a concelebrated Eucharist with seven priests — five men and Aquila and Priscilla.

- In the ninth century Pope Pascal I was Pope. His mother was called Theodora; in another catacomb Theodora is called: "Theodora Episcopa" — "Theodora the bishopess". Pope Pascal I was the son of a female bishop!

- Also in the ninth century was the English Pope John. He was really Joan. Pope Joan became pregnant and was deposed. Later archivists managed to airbrush her from church history.

- As late as the 1940s in Czechoslovakia, when the church ran out of priests a far-seeing Bishop Davidak ordained Ludmilla and several other women to the priesthood. Ludmilla is still living.

- St Thérèse of Lisieux, "The Little Flower" and Patron Saint of the Missions desired to be a priest. It is believed that she was secretly ordained. She said: "I feel in me the vocation to be a priest."

- The Bavarian mystic and stigmatist, Theresa Neumann, who died in 1962, is reputed to have been ordained in secret by a sympathetic bishop.

There is evidence in both Scripture and Tradition, the two sources of Divine Revelation for Catholics, that woman were and can be priests.

THERE IS THE STORY OF AN OLD LADY in her eighties who goes to confession and says to the priest: "I want to confess a serious sin of impurity." The priest is astounded and asks: "You're in your eighties and you committed a serious sin of impurity?" "Well actually, Father," continues the old lady, "it happened sixty years ago and I love to talk about it!"

If only all of us could approach our sexuality and religion with a little of that humour. But I know for certain that the guilt-ridden brainwashing about sex which I received in my teenage and young adult years marred my life. I was deeply unhappy, drowning in an ocean of badness and guilt. I felt dirty, unworthy and lost. I was not the only one. For hundreds of years now, poor ordinary people have suffered unbelievable repression and guilt. It has driven some insane. Some have even committed suicide. Our Church has a lot to answer for.

We should, on the other hand, actually thank God for our sexual pleasures. Just as we say "grace" before and after meals, we could say "grace" before and after sex:

Grace Before Sex

Heavenly Father, for the wonderful sexual pleasure we are about to receive from your loving hands we give you thanks and praise. May we always use our sexual powers in the pursuit and achievement of love. Amen.

IN DECEMBER 2001 THE BBC World Service carried a series of short radio programmes — at 4.30 in the morning! They were heard by my dear hermit friend Mother Frances. She knew about my preparations for this book and sent to the BBC for one of the programmes, entitled "Sex and the Soul". It made for fascinating listening. The programme quoted a few greats of spiritual history on the connection between sex, desire, the soul and the spiritual.

The thirteenth-century Dutch Christian mystic Hadewijch wrote of Christ her lover:

> My heart and my arteries and all my limbs palpitated and trembled with desire and as has often happened to me I felt myself being so fiercely tried that should I not give satisfaction to my lover, and should he not respond to my desire I would die of fury and die furious.

In another place she wrote: "I desire to know my lover wholly and to taste him in all his parts."

St Augustine gives further food for thought: "Love carries the flesh into the spirit and the spirit into the flesh." And then he says: "Give me a man in love. He knows what I mean. Give me one who is hungry. Give me one far away in this desert who thirsts and sighs for the springs of the eternal country. Give me that sort of man. He knows what I mean. But if I speak to a cold man he does not know what I'm talking about".

The programme went on to quote Guru Nanna, the founder of the Sikh faith, talking about finding God with the heart, passions, desires:

> My naive one,
> Why are you so vain?
> Why not celebrate the colours
> Within your own house?
> The bridegroom is very close to you.
> So, my silly girl,
> Why search outside ?
> If you paint your eyes
> With the eyeliners of awe,
> And adorn yourself well;
> Then you will be the true bride
> With whom the groom will stay in love.

Nik Douglas in his book *Spiritual Sex* looks at the ancient and modern connections between sex and spirituality from what he calls the point of view of Tantra: "Tantra maintains that sex is a sacred rite and that the same glorious power that produced your body can be invoked and directed to take control of your destiny." He quotes P.D. Ouspensky's

A New Model of the Universe: "Of all we know of life, only in sexual love is there a taste of ecstasy. Nothing else in our life brings us so near to the limits of human possibilities, beyond which begins the unknown."

Douglas deals with the important and absolutely true notion of sex as a sacrament:

> The core philosophy of Tantra is that sex is a sacrament, a sacred rite, a spiritual act. Most people are unaware that sex was viewed as a sacrament by many early Christians as well as by medieval Jewish mystics, that sacramental sex was once at the core of many other ancient spiritual traditions, and that the sacraments of sex and its secrets, which lead to personal power and spiritual liberation, are accessible to us in the present time. By viewing every act of sex as a spiritual rite or sacrament, we reconnect with the original source of our existence and empower our life with potent sacredness.

I agree totally with Douglas, but from a different perspective. Christianity has reduced the sacraments to either seven (if you are a Catholic) or two (if you are a Protestant). But there are thousands of sacraments — things that reveal the Divine to this world. Sex and sexuality are among the most important sacraments that we have.

I HAVE BEEN BLESSED with the number of people from around Ireland and further afield who have contacted me and written to me with very inspiring words and messages. I received the following beautiful prayer from "HW" in Kilkenny — a love letter from Jesus to us. He signed the prayer: "Dear Pat, Just a line to say thanks for being there. I hope you like this love letter and find it a comfort as I do."

A Love Letter

> I love you, I shed My own blood for you to make you clean. You are new! Believe it is true ! You are lovely in my eyes, and I created you to be just as you are. *Do not criticise yourself or be discouraged for not being perfect in your own eyes. This leads only to frustration. I want you to TRUST ME, one step, one day at a time.* Dwell in My power and love. Be free; be yourself. *Don't allow other people to run you. I will guide you if you let Me. Be aware of My Presence in*

everything. I give you love, joy and peace. Look to Me. I am your Shepherd and will lead you. *Follow Me only!* Listen and I will tell you My will. I love you, I love you! Let it flow from you — spill over to all you touch. *Be not concerned with yourself. You are My responsibility. I will change you.* You are to love yourself and love others simply because I love you. *Take your eyes off yourself. Look only at Me! I lead: I change: I make, but not when you are trying. I won't fight your efforts.* You are Mine. Let me have the joy of making you like Christ. Let me love you! Let me give you joy, peace and kindness. No one else can. Do you see? You are not your own. You have been bought with blood and now you belong to me. It is not your concern how I deal with you. Your only command is to look to Me and Me alone. Never to yourself and never to others. I love you. Do not struggle. Relax in My love. I know what is best and will do it with you, in you and through you. My will is perfect. My love is sufficient. I will supply all your needs. Look to Me! I love you, Jesus.

IT WOULD BE VERY WRONG for anybody, any Christian, to believe that he or she can have a spirituality without a morality. Our spirituality is our joy and our consolation. But we also have responsibilities — especially the two great moral responsibilities to love our God and to love our neighbour. It is one thing to have an enlightened liberal spirituality. That is freeing. But that does not mean that we can be "permissive" in the negative sense of that word. Each of us has the responsibility to do good and not wrong, to love and not to hurt. This applies in all aspects of our lives, including the sexual.

One of the basic yardsticks for the Christian life is the Ten Commandments. At the turn of the Millennium a national newspaper asked me to update the Ten Commandments. Of course I believe that God's Ten Commandments stand forever. But I don't think that God would mind me paraphrasing them slightly and proposing:

A Millennium Ten Commandments:

1. I am the Lord your God. I defy human understanding and delight in diversity. You shall each worship me according to your own lights.

2. All men and women of every time, place, colour and creed are my cherished sons and daughters. You shall not divide my people with your man-made doctrines.

3. Every day that dawns is a gift from me and a holy day. You shall keep all days holy by acts of love and service to each other.

4. Each person you know and meet is sent your way by me. Honour all your relationships as stepping stones to Heaven.

5. You shall not kill either the body or the soul. You shall abhor blind conformity and delight in individuality.

6. Your sexuality, with all its diversity and contradictions, is one of my greatest gifts. You shall not abuse this gift by separating it from love.

7. My justice is greater than human justice. You shall not deprive another, by your actions or inactions, of what is rightly theirs.

8. I am Truth. You shall conform all your thoughts, words and actions to that Truth.

9. When I sent you my Son you rejected him. You shall make atonement for that rejection by having a special love for all those whom the world rejects.

10. I reveal myself in creation. You shall cherish and preserve my universe, my world, my environment and my animals.

Part Three

Still a Thorn

Chapter Eleven

A Decade in My Life

"A time is coming when people will go mad, and when they meet someone who is not mad, they will turn to him and say: 'You are out of your mind', just because he is not like them."
— Abbot Anthony, Desert Father

I PUBLISHED A BOOK called *A Thorn in the Side* in 1994 and was very gratified that it was so popular and well-received. It could equally have been called *The Truth, and Nothing but the Truth, But Not the Whole Truth*. It wasn't that I told any untruths in that book; I didn't. But eleven years ago I still had a great deal of internal wrestling to do, especially about my sexuality, and I also was still in the process of getting help with that wrestling. So I was not ready then to deal with everything, especially with some the topics I address in this book. But *A Thorn In The Side* was a reasonable account of my life between 1952 and 1994.

While this current book is quite focused on my sexuality and spirituality, and I have already discussed my "coming out" in 1999, I do feel the need to write this chapter to bring the reader up to date with other important events in my life since 1994.

A Thorn in the Side, was, I think, successful. That success can be judged, I suppose, from the fact that it reached the top of *The Irish Times* paperback bestseller list. The book was also well reviewed on television and radio and in the press. It led to a number of important television appearances.

However *A Thorn in the Side* was not written to be a great worldly success or to make money. With all the bills I had (and indeed have), the book helped a little — but that was all. More important was its spiritual and human success. I had written the book because I was tired of doing quick three-minute interviews, where it is hardly possible to get a coherent view expressed, and because I was tired of the tabloid presentation of my life, ideas and times. I wanted to be able to put down, in one place, a comprehensive explanation of my life and a comprehensive expression of my beliefs and views. *A Thorn in the Side* did not do that perfectly, I'm sure. I was restrained by the lawyers who were afraid I would give anyone an opening to sue for libel. My natural inclination was and would be "publish and de damned".

I was very pleased by the great response I had from readers. I heard amusing reports of priests and nuns nervously buying the book. The book was available, by the way, from the Irish Catholic hierarchy-controlled shops — Veritas — which means truth!

I cannot remember getting any letter of abuse about the book. I'm sure that those who strongly disapprove of me simply did not buy it and therefore had no opinion to offer. But I had some lovely letters from people who enjoyed reading it and who were helped by it. I was so pleased that it helped people. I was especially pleased by the number of people who told me that they could go back to Mass and the Church after reading it. It made them feel that it was God that mattered rather than the church organisation and priests. This was especially true of marginalised groups like divorced Catholics and gay and lesbian Catholics.

I was also surprised at the number of people from outside Ireland who seemed to get it into their hands — from the United States, Australia, Africa . . . I had one letter from the Seychelles; a man found my book in a public toilet there, left by a previous occupant, and read it and wrote to me! I also heard from a number of priests and religious in different parts of the world who appreciated the book enough to write and congratulate me on my insight and courage.

It was a book written to get a lot off my chest and to help others — especially Catholics — to see their faith as a spiritual thing and to shake off the legalistic notion of faith.

ONE OF THE SPIN-OFFS of writing *A Thorn in the Side* was that it established my links with the highly successful Sunday newspaper, *The News of the World* (Irish edition). The newspaper serialised the book over two weeks and then offered me a permanent column, which has now lasted nearly eleven years. With hundreds of thousands of Irish readers, it is a great platform. What other Irish priest has such a big congregation every Sunday? I see the media and my column as a modern "pulpit". If the people will not come to you, then you go to the people. The column also assured me of a regular weekly income that has been very important. And I thoroughly enjoy the feedback I get from readers.

The column is meant to be topical and thought-provoking. So of course I get my bit of hate mail, as well as the letters of agreement. I get many more positive than negative letters. The *News of the World* people are very good about giving me editorial freedom and only occasionally have to watch me so that I do not stray into the libellous. I like to write about religion, society, politics, morality, life — anything that interests me. I have found my *News of the World* "handlers" very easy and honourable to deal with. I felt so comfortable with the paper that I was able to announce exclusively there that I had been ordained a bishop and, later still, that I was gay.

I have had some interesting trips with *News of the World* people. I have attended several Conservative and Labour Party conferences in Britain as part of the press brigade. And I had one interesting meeting with the British Chancellor, Gordon Brown.

I went to a London restaurant after midnight one night with several *News of the World* editors and staff. We noticed Gordon Brown, who was then Shadow Chancellor, at a nearby table with an attractive young woman. One of our editors, Bob Warren, spotted him and said that he would like to meet him and ask him to write a piece. I offered to take Bob's card and present it to the future Chancellor. I went to the table and asked him, "Excuse me, Mr Brown, would you mind if I spoke to you?" "Not at all, Father," he replied, noticing my clerical collar and my Irish accent. I continued, "I'm with *The News of the World*." His faced dropped. He was sure it was a set-up or a prank. The blood drained from his face. "We are up in the corner and Mr Warren was wondering if you'd join us for a moment." When he got his composure back, he agreed and we later had a good chat. He was very relieved that I was a real priest and that we were not a crowd of *News of the World* hacks out looking for a scalp! The story is still told with great relish in *News of the World* circles.

THE LATE FR MICHAEL CLEARY was, in my opinion, one of the greatest cynics and hypocrites I have ever come across. I regret that I have to express my opinion so forcefully, but that is the lasting impression I am left with. In spite of that, I am sure that he has made his peace with God, received mercy and is in Heaven.

For decades Michael Cleary had a live-in partner who mothered children for him. She was a decent woman called Phyllis Hamilton. I only met Phyllis late in her life when she was dying of cancer. I found her to be a lovely woman, while Ross, her son by Fr Cleary, is a very bright young man. As somebody who, through no fault of his own, found himself betrayed by the Church, I felt a very strong empathy for him. But the day I met him he was, quite rightly, full of anger for the Catholic Church and for priests and did not treat me very warmly.

Right up until the day he died Fr Cleary introduced Phyllis to everybody as: "This is Phyllis, a young unmarried mother I took pity on and allowed to live with me." The truth was that Cleary had seduced Phyllis after she went to him as a priest for advice and help and from then on she shared his bed, provided for at least some of his sexual needs and mothered his children.

Fr Cleary was, in my opinion, a "hit man" for the Irish Catholic Church and bishops. If there was dirty work to be done Cleary was despatched to do it. When Fr Michael Keane, the Mayo priest and founder of the Knock Marriage Bureau was unjustly sacked from his parish, Fr Michael Cleary was sent to "reason" with him. Fr Keane couldn't stand him. Cleary came at poor Fr Keane with politics, lies, pretence and injustice. Thankfully Fr Keane had the good sense to tell Cleary in no uncertain terms to get lost.

I was involved in another case in which Cleary was caught up — the case of Sheila. Sheila was in a long-term relationship with a young Dublin curate, Fr Des Murtagh, a classmate of my own. The thing was becoming public. Cleary was despatched once again; he sent Des Murtagh into hiding. He convinced poor Sheila that Murtagh was in the US waiting and sent her away, unknowingly giving him power of attorney over the house and bank accounts which Sheila and the priest shared together as a couple. When she was away Cleary unsuccessfully tried to sell the house from under her. Sheila went through mental torture and a breakdown. Cleary made life hell for her for as long as he could.

It came my turn to be targeted by Cleary. The Church didn't and doesn't approve of the marriages I perform. Cleary wrote a column about this in *The Irish Catholic* making me out to be a "con man". I was astonished when I read the article. I rang him at home. He was having his tea at the time. He deliberately chewed his tea loudly into the telephone and said: "Well, it's like this, son. When Jesus was hanging on the cross he had no right of reply. You will just have to offer it up like him." And then he hung up. *The Irish Catholic* refused to allow me the right of reply.

The next attack on me from Cleary came on his nightly radio show on Dublin's 98FM. In an hour-long programme, he claimed that my marriages were "con jobs" and that I was a "con man". I heard of the broadcast and asked the station to keep a copy of the show. Cleary and the station refused me a right of reply. So I sued for libel.

We spent three weeks in the High Court in Dublin. My senior barrister, Michael McDowell TD, the current Irish Minister for Justice, pulled out of the case the night before it started because of an important vote in the Dáil. I ended up with Eamon de Valera, a good barrister but not the kind of streetfighter I needed. I was up against Cleary, 98FM and, as it turned out, the Catholic hierarchy. I knew that I was going to get law but not so sure I was going to get justice.

By the time the case came for hearing Michael Cleary had died; so it was really 98FM versus me. The Catholic Church turned out in force to support the radio station. The Professor of Canon Law at Maynooth, Dr John McAreavy, now the Bishop of Dromore, gave evidence against me. The parish priest of Larne, where I live, Fr Archie Molloy, came out on the side of 98FM, as did the present parish priest of Lisburn, Fr Sean Rogan. Fr Molloy appeared confused and nervous and had little to add. Fr Rogan seemed to be more hostile. He talked of all the people I had hurt and led astray. My barrister asked him for the name and address of one of those I had hurt. Fr Rogan could not offer one name or address. But it was important for the jury to see a parade of priests against the dissident!

My book *A Thorn in the Side* was ripped to bits — all out of context of course. I fought as best I could. But I soon realised that I was up against not only 98FM but the full weight of the Catholic Church with all their money, influence, power and friends in the "establishment". I was very lucky not to lose. I ended up with a hung jury. So there had to be a retrial.

Before the retrial I appointed two wonderful men for the new trial — solicitor Padraic Ferry and Senior Counsel Adrian Hardiman, who is now a judge of the Irish Supreme Court. Walking in with Hardiman and Ferry was a different ballgame. Within two days the case was settled. My legal fees were paid and I received a modest lump sum. But I had won the day and the principle.

I believe Fr Michael Cleary would have been capable of doing anything in the name of the Catholic Church and in the name of God. There are still a number of Michael Clearys in the Irish Catholic Church today. Some of them are more subtle and hidden. I'm sure that there are even a few Clearys in preparation. May the Lord protect us from them and from the harm they do! The most dangerous of them masquerade as liberal and friendly — the Fr Trendy types. Beware the smiling, hand-wringing, patronising, liberal-talking, singing priest!

MY OLDEST NEPHEW, Christopher Geoghegan, the son of my sister Margaret, took his own young life. He was only twenty-three years old.

Christopher had always been something of a loner and a brooder. Like a lot of young people in Dublin and elsewhere, he became involved in drug-taking. It created havoc in his life and in his family. But he seemed to have beaten his habit. He was working as a printer and had his own flat. Then, one week, he went missing for days and the gardaí were notified. They broke into his flat and sadly they found him lying dead in bed. He had used a shotgun to kill himself.

Why did he do it? We do not really know. How did he come to have a shotgun? We think he may have been minding it for some criminal, perhaps a drug pusher and gangster.

Obviously his mother Margaret, his dad Christy and all his family and friends were devastated. I was to do his funeral — at his mother's request. But Cardinal Desmond Connell refused to let me say the funeral Mass. Not even under the circumstances of a family tragedy was Connell willing to put the Gospel compassion of Jesus before his legalistic Roman Catholicism. His hardness of heart hurt us all. My understanding is that Bishop Brendan Comiskey of Wexford (to whom I had appealed) and one or two other bishops prevailed upon Connell to be compassionate. But they failed to penetrate his self-righteous legalism.

So we had no place to hold Christopher's funeral Mass. I went on the Gay Byrne radio programme and appealed for a church. We had two offers. One was from the Church of Ireland in Dawson Street, who offered to allow the funeral — but I could not be the main celebrant. The absolutely generous, unconditional offer came from the Unitarian Church on St Stephen's Green. They just flung their doors open to us and told us to do what we wanted.

We experienced no Christianity from Cardinal Connell and the Archdiocese of Dublin. We received conditional Christianity from the

Church of Ireland. But we received total Christianity from the wonderful Unitarians.

CARDINAL CAHAL DALY managed to write his memoirs *Steps on a Pilgrim Way* and not even mention me, even though the most public dispute of his lifetime was with me when he sacked me as a priest of the Diocese of Down and Connor! He has been asked about this omission several times in the media and answers with a mixture of discomfort, anger and silence. Personally, I never want to be accused of not addressing any issue in my life, even though sometimes it would be easier not to. The gain and loss of St Andrew's Church in Omeath, County Louth, was an experience of joy turning to pain.

In 1997, I spotted St Andrew's for sale. That night, I happened to be having a meal with two friends and parishioners, Arthur and Margaret McIntyre. They headed the multi-million pound pet food superstore chain, Jollyes. To cut a long story short, Arthur decided to buy St Andrew's and renovate it. Arthur, a religious man, wanted to be married there religiously himself. Margaret was his third wife and they had only been married civilly.

The "arrangement among friends" was that the Jollyes would lend the £120,000 for the purchase and renovation of St Andrews to Crimish Ltd, a company set up to own and run the church. Arthur, Margaret and I were the three directors of Crimish, while Margaret and I would each have fifty per cent shareholdings. Couples using the church for weddings would pay £200 to the McIntyres via Crimish — £100 towards the annual running costs of the church and £100 off the capital layout. Eventually the interest-free loan would be paid off and I would own the church. In the meantime, Margaret left her fifty per cent share to me in a new will. We had a wonderful opening ceremony in April 1998. I presented Arthur and Margaret with a Waterford cut-glass church as a gesture of gratitude.

Sadly the friendship between myself and the McIntyres broke down. They withdrew as parishioners, supporters and patrons and they demanded that the church be sold. I prayed about it; I had no interest in having a big battle with them. I could not afford all the lawyers they could afford. Eventually, I came to the same conclusion as Job in the Bible: "The Lord has given. The Lord has taken away. Blessed be the Name of the Lord."

I now have the use of a church in Dublin, which is much more convenient for couples from the Republic of Ireland. But it is strange how life can change and change so drastically and quickly. Arthur and Mags McIntyre are now divorced and, on New Year's Eve, 31 December 2004, I celebrated Arthur's fourth marriage — to my sister Linda — in Dublin. What was that old Irish saying? "It's a long road that has no turning."

"MAN PROPOSES, GOD DISPOSES." Since Cardinal Daly unjustly sacked me from the Diocese of Down and Connor, he has always refused to meet me or share a media platform with me. But God has His own ways — and His own wonderful sense of humour!

I had been to London for a television discussion show. I had flown Belfast–Heathrow, but I had to fly back to Dublin for a meeting. The television company, Carlton, booked me on an Aer Lingus flight — business class! As I was descending the ramp to board the plane, a smiling Aer Lingus attendant said: "Hello Father, you're travelling with the Cardinal today." I thought that he was joking, as I often get people joking with me about my relationship with the Irish Catholic hierarchy.

Sure enough, there was Cardinal Daly sitting in the front row — and they had put me sitting in the same row, with just one seat separating us. He nearly died when he saw me. He ignored me and kept reading his breviary. I stretched out my hand but he ignored it. I caught the fleshy part of the side of his hand and shook it anyway. He looked furious.

After a little while, a very attractive young woman sat in the empty seat between us. She removed her jacket, threw off her high-heel shoes and opened her blouse slightly — making herself comfortable for the plane journey. After a little while we struck up a conversation. "Are you a priest?" she inquired. "Indeed I am," I replied. "Well," she said, "what do you think of all these bonking bishops?" She was referring to Bishop Eamon Casey, who was in the news at the time. I was highly amused. Cardinal Daly was shifting uncomfortably in his seat. I slipped the woman a note which read: "The guy the other side is the Cardinal." That only made her worse. "Are you afraid of women?" she asked. "Absolutely not," I said. "I was brought up with six sisters." "Good," she said, "will you come on a date with me when I'm next in Belfast?" "If you're paying, of course I will," I played along. We then agreed on a meal in Paul Rankin's famous restaurant on Belfast's Great Victoria Street. Cardinal Daly looked unbelievably uncomfortable. If Aer Lingus had had parachutes, I'm sure he would have baled out there and then.

All in all, it was a very funny flight. Cardinal Daly had sworn never to meet me, but God threw us together in the air — and in the company of an enticing young woman. Now tell me that God does not have a sense of humour!

ON 19 MAY 1998, AT 4.00 PM, I was consecrated a bishop in The Oratory, Prince's Gardens, Larne, County Antrim, by Tridentine Bishop Michael Cox. In the press statement I released at the time, I fully explained the occasion and my reasons for embracing the episcopacy at that stage in my life. I explained how I saw my role as a priest as providing a ministry for those who had been rejected by the "official church", and that I now wanted to extend and pass on my ministry to others through ordination. I identified the particular groups of people for whom I saw my ministry as a refuge from their alienation at the hands of the hierarchy:

- Divorced Catholics and Christians needing remarriage and the separated.
- Mixed religion couples needing neutral Christian ceremonies.
- Priests who have left or priests who want to marry and remain priests.

- Couples who want to use their consciences on issues like contraception.

- The more than five thousand women who are excommunicated every year in Ireland for having an abortion. (Personally I am anti-abortion.)

- Women who are in relationships with priests. I have already 110 such women in our support group "Bethany".

- The gay, lesbian and trans-gendered community.

- Women denied power and Holy Orders within the Church.

- The victims of sexual and physical abuse in the church who are denied proper counselling and compensation.

- The children of priests and bishops.

- People who are arbitrarily refused marriage annulments after a five- to ten-year wait.

- Children (especially in Northern Ireland) in non-Catholic schools who are refused First Holy Communion and Confirmation.

- The increasing numbers of children who are being bullied in schools when they or their parents are ignored by the church authorities, school managers and boards of governors.

- Young student priests who are expelled from seminaries and never given a reason.

- And generally people who are hurt and wounded by harsh and thoughtless administrative decisions within the institutional and hierarchical church.

In my press statement, I went on to point out how I was fully "qualified" to become a bishop by "becoming the pastor/shepherd of a church or faith community" (my two communities at Larne and Omeath); and by "having another validly consecrated bishop lay hands on you and invoke the Holy Spirit by way of the Prayer of

Consecration and thereby receive the 'Apostolic Succession'". The validity of Bishop Michael Cox, who consecrated me, has been recognised by the Roman Catholic Archdiocese of Dublin, who have urged him to apply for laicisation. His validity has also been attested to by Dr Willie Walsh, Bishop of Killaloe. The bishop who consecrated Bishop Cox, Bishop Broadberry, was laicised by Dr Donal Herlihy, the Bishop of Ferns, some years ago — after he consecrated Bishop Cox — his validity obviously being accepted. Like all laicised bishops and priests, Bishop Broadberry remains a bishop and must dispense the Sacraments in danger of death.

Every valid bishop can trace his lineage back through former generations and eventually back to the Apostles. That is why we then talk about the important notion of "Apostolic Succession". The following is my Episcopal lineage through Bishop Cox:

- Patrick Buckley; consecrated by
- Michael Cox; consecrated by
- Kieran Broadberry (later laicised); consecrated by
- Clemente Dominquez Gomez; consecrated by
- Pierre Martin Ngo Dinh Thuc of the Vatican.

So my Episcopal validity goes straight back to the Vatican itself.

The reasons for choosing consecration at that time were many and varied. Firstly, my conscience dictated that it was God's Will; it was not a course I entered into lightly, but only following much soul-searching and spiritual advice and direction from close advisors. Secondly, a number of priests and lay people had approached me, unsolicited, and asked to minister with me. Thirdly, at that time I had been threatened with suspension and excommunication if I didn't stop my ministry; I saw such unwarranted threatening as a "sign". When the threats didn't work I was offered the possibility of negotiations and an oral but legally binding deal that would have left me financially secure and would have given me a position and status within the

Church — but at the price of stopping my ministry and silence. I felt that I could not allow my conscience to be bowed by either threats or enticements and therefore I was embarking on a broadened ministry.

WHILE FULLY ACCEPTING AND ACKNOWLEDGING the validity of Bishop Cox, his later activities, which included the ordaining of singer Sinéad O'Connor, made me extremely uneasy.

I agree with the ordination of women; I have already said so earlier in the book, and I myself have ordained Mother Frances, as I discuss below. And who are we to contend that Sinéad O'Connor did not have a vocation? But I was unhappy about the circumstances surrounding Sinéad's ordination. Firstly, a cheque for £80,000 was in circulation. Bishop Cox later said that he returned the cheque to Sinéad. I was very afraid of simony — the buying of holy orders. Traditionally in the Church, simony invalidates those orders. Secondly, I think that Sinéad should have prepared for priesthood by going on a retreat and entering on a course of scripture, theology and spirituality.

I wish Bishop Cox and Sinéad well. In fact, I know that Sinéad is a wonderfully kind and charitable person. However, I did not wish to be overly identified with Bishop Cox's perspective. As a result of this, I felt it necessary to align myself with another valid bishop. So on 14 February 1999, Bishop Peter Paul Brennan of the US Ecumenical Catholic Church performed a conditional consecration for me. His lineage is both solid and interesting; Bishop Brennan's Holy Orders go back to: Cardinal Antonio Barberini, nephew of Pope Urban VIII; through him, Cardinal Scipione Rebiba, Patriarch of Constantinople; and through him, Pope Benedict XIII. You can't get more Catholic and valid than that!

ON 5 OCTOBER 2000 the Deputy Chief Herald of Ireland issued me with my Episcopal coat of arms — as he does to all bishops. That coat of arms consists of the following elements:

- The traditional green Episcopal hat with the three lines of golden tassels.
- Three bulls — the arms of the Buckleys.
- A black sheep with a bishop's crosier imposed, symbolising that I am a "black shepherd" for the black sheep.
- A priest's stole with my Episcopal motto: *Tolerance, Love, Diversity*.

I believe that this coat of arms and motto sums up my ministry.

FOR YEARS NOW I HAVE HAD a spiritual dilemma. Should I stay as part of the Roman Catholic Church or should I, with others of like mind, "break away" and form our own church and call it "The Liberal Catholic Church of Ireland" or "The Independent Catholic Church" or "The Celtic Catholic Church" or whatever? My fears about going down this latter route are threefold.

- I do not want to be on any kind of ego trip, setting up my own little "empire". I only want to discern and do God's will.
- I do not want to become a Catholic Ian Paisley, starting up a Free Catholic Church.
- I do not want to further splinter Christianity. We have too many churches as it is.

I am not sure what will happen in the future. Certainly, if I and those I work with feel that God is calling us to become "independent", I would do so. Like many others, I now believe that the Roman Catholic institution and hierarchy is rotten and intrinsically evil. But what do you do? Do you stay in — even marginally in — and change it from the inside or do you shake the dust off your feet and leave?

So, for now, we have established a little society called The Oratory Society. I like the word *oratory* because it is neutral and for prayer and marriages, it allows people of all kinds to come. We are also inspired a bit by the oratory thinking and movement of the great Cardinal John Henry Newman, who was a great champion of conscience. He has said: "I will drink to conscience first and afterwards to the Pope"; and "Conscience is the aboriginal Vicar of Christ".

So The Oratory Society is a collection of priests, religious, hermits and lay people who want to be spiritual as Christian and Catholic but who want their conscience respected. We are just a baby society. We are learning as we go. We are on a journey. Hopefully we are led on that journey by the Holy Spirit.

I HAD THE IMMENSE PRIVILEGE of ordaining Frances Meigh (known affectionately and respectfully as Mother Frances) to the priesthood on 14 September 1998.

Frances began life as an Anglican but converted to Catholicism in her early twenties. She wanted to become a nun at that age but was pushed towards marriage by a gruff confessor and spiritual director. But all along, Frances's call was to the active/contemplative spiritual life.

Frances did marry and had three children. Later her marriage was annulled by the Church. As far as the Church is concerned, she had never been married. She wittily proclaims, "I am an unmarried mother!"

By that time Frances had completed an MA degree and was a member of the Royal College of Art. In her early career, Frances worked as a newspaper cartoonist and as a portrait artist. She later developed her iconography for which she is now so highly regarded. Frances then went to Calcutta for a number of years and did Trojan work there in collaboration with Mother Teresa and Dr Jack Preger. She wrote a book about her Indian experiences, *The Jack Preger Story*, which was later to become a Channel 4 television film.

All along Frances had never lost her vocation to the religious life and the life of contemplation. She spent some time at Syon Abbey in the south of England where she discerned that her true vocation was to be a hermit. She pursued her hermetic calling in Whitby in the north of England. In 1994 she had a spiritual revelation in which she knew that she was called to be a priest and to offer daily Mass for the suffering world.

After my consecration as Bishop in 1998, she contacted me and we met. I knew immediately that this woman was authentic and spiritually true. Between July and September 1998 we kept in very regular touch and Frances was ordained on 14 September. Her ordination made world news.

Since her ordination Frances has served at St Andrew's in Omeath and at The Hermitage in Forkhill, Armagh. With the closure of St Andrew's, Mother Frances lives and ministers exclusively now at Forkhill. In late 2001, Frances converted part of her cosy hermitage into a chapel — The Chapel of the Suffering World. She says Mass there daily and is sought out by scores of people for spiritual direction and pastoral help. Since moving to live in South Armagh she has painted some icons on the theme *The God of Both Sides*.

I regard Frances as the gem in our crown. She is a loyal friend and advisor but above all else a powerhouse of prayer for The Oratory Society. Frances has made history by becoming ordained a priest. In time to come she will be seen as a pioneer and a prophetess.

I WAS DRIVING THROUGH DUBLIN one lunchtime in September 2000. I noticed a young man in his early twenties dressed in black with all his belongings in a black plastic bag at his feet, standing at a traffic light with a placard that read, "Homeless. Please Help."

I reached £3 through my car window and a voice with a soft English accent responded, "God bless ye, sur." I was gob-smacked — it was as though a character from Dickens had just spoken to me. I was intrigued. I parked and invited the young man to speak to me. Initially he was cautious, quite rightly. He had been approached a lot on the streets of Dublin by weirdoes. It was common for him to be offered money for sex by older males. I sat in my car with the window down and he sat on his black bag on the footpath. He told me that he was from the Peak District of England, that he was a drug addict and that he was wanted by the police back home. He was spending up to £1,000 a week on heroin in Dublin.

I gave him some more money and said I would keep in touch with him. He was sleeping on the street but the girls in the box office of the Gaiety Theatre in Dublin allowed him to use that address. He used a false name — Francis Gilberthorpe — but I will call him "Tim" here.

I wrote to him a few times but as I expected I received no answer. But on my next visit to Dublin I found him under a dirty blanket on the street. I brought him for a burger and chips. At the end of the lunch, he told me he wanted to beat heroin and asked if I would help him. I gladly agreed.

I spent all day telephoning and calling to rehabilitation centres. Everywhere there was a six-month waiting list. I asked for methadone so that I could detox Tim myself. Nobody would give me what I needed. Later that night I hailed a taxi and asked the driver to take me to whatever part of Dublin the heroin dealers operated in. The driver was shocked at such a request from a priest. I made a deal to buy the methadone I needed, illegally, for £40 the next morning!

But during the night I had a fear that I might get bad or impure methadone and do Tim harm. So I needed a plan B. I telephoned RTÉ Radio and spoke to the Marian Finucane Programme. They allowed me to go on the air and appeal for methadone and help for Tim. An hour later, as I was about to buy the illegal methadone from a pusher, my mobile telephone rang. I was being promised perfectly legal and good quality methadone. It would arrive by post!

I brought Tim home with me to Larne. After soaking himself in the bath he occupied our guest room. I detoxed him over ten days. And then he stayed with us until Christmas when he went home to see his family.

He has stayed in England. He is drug-free after eleven years. He is working as a stock control clerk. He has sorted out his problems with the police. A few months ago he arrived back to see me — a transformed young man in his business suit. He stood in my sitting room and said: "I'm back to thank you for saving my life." Hearing those words was better than winning the lottery. Encounters with people like Tim give my life and my priesthood such profound meaning. "As long as you did it to one of these, the least of my brethren, you did it to me."

ON 6 JUNE 2001 I celebrated the Silver Jubilee of my ordination. We celebrated with a concelebrated Mass in the Unitarian Church on St Stephen's Green in Dublin and a reception afterwards in a nearby hotel. Achieving my twenty-fifth anniversary was very important for me and I felt that, no matter what happens from now on, at least I had given twenty-five years of faithful service.

As a teenager and a seminarian I used to pray to God to allow me to be ordained, even if I died the next day. That is now thirty-five years ago. I'm very glad that in spite of all the ups and downs of being a dissident I am still around as a Catholic Christian and a priest.

I received lots of wonderful gifts from loving people for my jubilee. But one gift was unusual. One of my former teachers — Mr Gerard Tuohy, my history and geography teacher from the College of Commerce, Rathmines, attended the jubilee Mass. On the way out he handed me a gift. When I opened it, I was amazed to discover it was my European history book from February 1970 — thirty-one years previously. I was amazed that he had kept it, given all the students he has had before and since. He wittily replied: "I kind of regard it as a second-class relic."

With gratitude in my heart for the gift of the last quarter of a century, I now head into a new quarter in a spirit of faith, hope and a good helping of God-given optimism.

Chapter Twelve

THE FUTURE

"We have all harboured fantasies, usually inspired by fictional characters, of stepping into the shoes of a hero, the main man or woman. Of course, the fantasies come without the reality of living in the solitary and spirit-breaking role of the maverick. We have all wanted to be a Serpico, a Woodward or a Bernstein without the price that has to be paid in risk or the consequences of something going horribly wrong."
— Michael Sheridan, Sunday Independent, *30 June 1996*

I LOVE THAT QUOTE. Many people fantasise about being a hero in life or about playing the leading role. But for most people, it is only a fantasy. Firstly, they would not really want their comfortable lives disturbed. Secondly, they would not have the strength and courage to be a maverick or a hero and experience the isolation and pressure that the role can bring.

Some people in the Church, the media and the "establishment" have, over the years, cynically and insultingly called me a maverick. Am I a maverick? *Chamber's Dictionary* says that a maverick is "an individual who does not conform; a determined individualist". I am certainly a non-conformist and a determined individualist. I believe that rules and structures are important in society and in the church; otherwise there would be anarchy. But I think that those rules have to be both intelligent and flexible. I can be very happy as a member of a team — but it has to be a team that respects both conformity and individuality. God has given us all an intelligence and, more importantly, a conscience. He would not have given us those things if He did not want us to use them. So there can be general norms in life that help regulate the community. But the general norms must be applied to the individual's own life through the use of his intelligence and his conscience. I would like once again to repeat the words of the great Cardinal John Henry Newman: "Conscience is the aboriginal Vicar of Christ." In other words, the most important pope is your conscience.

One of the things I have had to put up with over the years is black propaganda from the Catholic Church and its spokespersons. This is most often done in not-to-be-quoted whispers. For years now, they have tried to convince journalists that I am mad. But as St John Vianney's bishop said to those who accused Vianney of the same thing: "I wish the rest of you were half as mad!"

Nobody in the Irish Catholic hierarchy is willing to come on live media and have a debate with me. It seems they have been advised that the best way to deal with me is to say "no comment". Why do they not want to debate the truth openly? I have even offered to go on TV on my own and face the forty Irish bishops and their cleverest advisors. But fifty of them will not face one of me! Why? What are they afraid of? I think they must know that many of their positions would not stand up to intelligent, rational and Bible-based debate and scrutiny.

So maybe I am a maverick. But if I am, and I say this fully conscious of all my failings, I am God's maverick. Was Jesus not a maverick? Did not the Pharisees accuse him of being a non-conformist and a determined individualist? My enemies will jump at these words and say: "There, you see, he thinks he's another Jesus." Cardinal Daly once accused me of having a "saviour complex". But I thought that we Christians and we priests were supposed to be *"alter Christus"* — other Christs. That was drummed into me in the seminary. Of course, Jesus was sinless. I will never be anything but a struggling sinner. But I still must *strive* to be "another Jesus".

I THINK THAT THE ONLY WAY not to make enemies is never to make anything or do nothing! Wasn't it Swetchine who said: "In order to have an enemy one must be somebody." Years ago I came across a lovely little poem by Charles Mackay called "No Enemies?"

> You have no enemies, you say?
> Alas, my friend, the boast is poor;
> He who has mingled in the fray
> Of duty, that the brave endure,
> *Must* have made foes! If you have none,
> Small is the work that you have done.
> You've hit no traitor on the hip,
> You've dashed no cup from perjured lip,
> You've never turned the wrong to right,
> You've been a coward in the fight.

Since Cardinal Cahal Daly sacked me I have been treated as a leper by the Catholic Church, its hierarchy and many of the clergy. I have experienced great opposition. I have had to face the wrath of the Catholic hierarchy and the clergy for more than twenty years now. I have had numerous difficulties created for me by people from all walks of life who want to please the hierarchy and who resent me for being non-establishment. I am unwelcome in some newspapers and media outlets. I have found that one branch of the establishment winks at another branch, whether they be church establishment, media establishment, medical establishment, civil service, business, etc.

I should not be surprised that I experience opposition. My greatest hero said: "If they persecuted me they will persecute you. Wherever the Master is the servant must also be." Once again, it is a case of the Scribes and the Pharisees. And these new ones would crucify Jesus just as surely today as their predecessors did in their day.

I see opposition as a sign that I am on the right road. If I had no opposition I would be on a wrong road. The great Gandhi said: "If a million people follow you; ask yourself: "Where have I gone wrong?"

I AM SOMETIMES ASKED, "What's your master plan?" My answer is, "My master plan is to follow the Master's plan." I am not being smart when I say this. Life is a journey; we never know where it will take us. If any of us look back over the last ten or twenty years of our life I think we can say that we never envisaged our life taking the shape it did. As a teenager, I wanted to be a priest in a Dublin parish, to be near family. I never thought that my journey to and through priesthood would take me from Dublin, to Waterford, to Wales, to Northern Ireland. More importantly, I never thought that my journey would take me from being a narrow-minded conservative young seminarian to being a public full-blown radical and dissident priest and bishop. You could say that being a comfortable, full-of-certainty priest was in my original "master plan". But the Master's plan was that I should go on a much different journey; a journey, for all its pains and challenges, that has been most wonderfully rewarding and satisfying.

One of the things I love about my life is that no day is the same. One day I am writing my newspaper column. Another day, I am celebrating a wedding or a gay blessing. Another day, I am detoxing a heroin addict. Another day still, I am defending my work and my views on radio and television. Variety is the spice of life. The word "diversity" is on my Episcopal coat of arms. How bored I'd be in a middle-class Dublin parish reading out nonsensical pastoral letters from an archbishop!

So my master plan is to try, through prayer and the circumstances of my life, to discern God's will for me and then try to do it. I am on a fascinating and lifelong mystery tour. But I know two things with absolute certainty. I have God as a travelling companion and my final destination is Heaven.

People ask me: "How do you know that you are saved and going to Heaven?" I know it because of what my thirty-three-year-old Saviour did for me on the first Good Friday. He has purchased the tickets. I simply have to turn up, and turn up I will. Of course I must live my life in conformity with the gift I have been given.

It also helps to remember that we are not in control of everything in our own destiny. I love those words of Archbishop Oscar Romero, another church "maverick", a martyr in fact, whom the Vatican will be slow to canonise in case it upsets some of the Catholic despots of South America:

Prophets of a Future Not Our Own

It helps, now and then, to step back and take the long view.
The Kingdom is not only beyond our efforts, it is beyond our vision.

We accomplish in our lifetime only a tiny fraction of the magnificent
enterprise that is God's work.
Nothing we do is complete, which is another way of saying that the
Kingdom is beyond us.

No statement says all that could be said.
No prayer fully expresses our faith.
No confession brings perfection.
No pastoral visit brings wholeness.
No programme accomplishes the Church's mission.
No set of goals and objectives include everything.

That is what we are about: we will plant seeds that
one day will grow.
We water seeds already planted,
knowing that they hold future promise.
We lay foundations that will need further development.
We provide yeast that produces facts beyond our capabilities.

We cannot do everything, and that is liberation.
This enables us to do something, and to do it very well.
It may be incomplete, but it is a beginning, a step along the way,
An opportunity for God's grace to enter and do the rest.

We may never see the end results,
But that is the difference between the master builder and the worker.
We are workers, not master builders,
Ministers, not messiahs.

We are prophets of a future not our own.
Amen.

I believe that I am a prophet; I was anointed one at my baptism way back in 1952. But thankfully I do not have to make up or preach my message. God is in me and I am a prophet of a message and a future that is not my own.

I can also identify with that other South American priest prophet, Archbishop Helder Camara, another "maverick", who wrote:

> There is a danger of losing your head when simple people begin to think of you as an extraordinary man, as a saint. But there fortunately are ways of guarding against it. For example, when I am about to go out and face a huge audience which is applauding me and cheering me, I turn to Christ and say to him simply: "Lord, this is Your triumphal entry into Jerusalem! I am just the little donkey You are riding on!" And it's true.

I WANT TO CONCLUDE by stating the obvious, but only because sometimes the obvious is the best thing to say: I am different and I have always been different.

Maybe the reason that people think I am a maverick is because I am different from run-of-the-mill priests. I have never been able to be part of the cosy clubs of this life — and that includes the cosy clerical club.

I like country and western music. It is emotional. I love that Jim Reeves song that says: "This world is not my home; I'm just a-passin' through." I feel that emotion very deeply. I believe that I belong to another world. I believe that I belong to eternity. I love this world and I love life but my spirit is restless for my true home. I feel like the people of Israel. When they were in captivity in Babylon their captors asked them to sing. They answered: "How can we sing the Lord's song in this alien place?"

Ever since I came to the mixed religion society that is Northern Ireland in 1978, fundamental Protestants have challenged me about being a Catholic. For many of them, Catholics are not Christians and will not be "saved" or go to Heaven. When I am asked, "Mr Buckley, have you been saved?" I always answer, "Yes, of course I have." Then they asked me when was I saved. Many of them can tell you the date, time and place of their saving! But I always answer and say, "I was saved on the first Good Friday when the thirty-three-year-old Son of God and my loving Brother died for me on Calvary." And that's exactly what I believe. I don't even *believe* that I am going to Heaven; I *know* I am! Not because of what I have done, but because of what Jesus has done for me. I am saved and I must strive every day to live the life of a "saved" man by loving my God and my neighbour.

I have always been greatly consoled by the last two lines of the hymn composed by St Alphonsus (1696–1787), "O Bread of Heaven":

> For how can he deny me Heaven
> Who here on earth Himself hath given?

THIS IS WHAT I BELIEVE will happen to me when I go before God to be judged. I believe I will stand naked and alone before God. Gathered all around will be the people of all times and places, including my family, friends and all those who knew me in life. God will ask the Recording Angel to read out the very long list of my lifetime's sins. As the angel goes through the list my face will blush a deeper and deeper red.

When the angel is finished speaking there will be a stunning silence. Then God will say, "Has anyone any good thing to say about this man?" A man on the left will stand up and say: "Lord, I was thumbing a lift to Dublin one day and he stopped and gave me a lift." Then a woman on the right will stand and say: "Lord, my children and I had no food and heat one night and he brought us a box of groceries and a tank of gas." Then a young man will stand and say: "Lord, I was in prison one time and my family disowned me and he came to see me and put some money into my tuck shop account." Then another young man will stand and say: "Lord, I was a heroin addict and he brought me home and detoxed me." Then an old woman will stand and say: "Lord, the government cut off my health benefits and he represented me at an appeal tribunal and got me back on benefit." And so on.

Then there will be another stunning silence. Then the Lord will say: "Pat, though your sins are like scarlet I will make them as white as snow. I was hungry and you gave me food. I was thirsty and you gave me drink. I was naked and you clothed me. I was sick and you visited me. I was in prison and you came to see me. I was a stranger and you made me welcome. Come take possession of the place reserved for you by the Father since the beginning of time."

Epilogue

For me, thank God, the genie of my sexuality is out of the bottle and won't go back in. Through God's grace, I have begun to connect sexuality and spirituality. I am only beginning that journey but what an exciting prospect it is! And my Church genie has escaped too. No longer do I fear men or doctrines. God is my guide as is my God-given conscience.

I would like to quote one more poem, written by the Sufi poet Mirabai (translated by Robert Bly):

Why Mira Can't Go Back to Her Old House

The colours of the Dark One have penetrated Mira's body;
All the other colours washed out.
Making love with the Dark One and eating little, those are
My pearls and my carnelians.
Meditation beads and the forehead streak, those are my
Scarves and my rings.
That's enough feminine wiles for me.
My teacher taught me this.
Approve me or disapprove me: I praise the Mountain
Energy
Night and day.
I take the path that ecstatic human beings have taken for
Centuries.
I don't steal money, I don't hit anyone.
What will you charge me with?
I have felt the swaying of the elephant's shoulders;
And now you want me to climb on a jackass?
Try to be serious.

I have experienced the True God, the Living God. I have felt the swaying of the Divine Elephant's shoulders. I can never again ride the jackass of the institutional Church with its saddle of oppression and its blinkers of guilt.

But I am happy to be a Catholic Christian, priest and bishop. I have thrown away the dirty water of ecclesiastical tyranny but retained the precious baby of faith and spirituality.

I hope that this book might help some of my brothers and sisters in the world as they make their often painful pilgrimage from slavery to freedom.

Recommended Further Reading

Allison, James, *Faith Beyond Resentment: Fragments Gay and Catholic*, 2001, London: Darton, Longman and Todd, ISBN: 0-232-52411-4.

Alison, James, *On Being Liked: Intellectual Dynamite and Spiritual Joy*, 2003, London: Darton, Longman and Todd, ISBN: 0-232-52517-X.

Boswell, John, *Rediscovering Gay History: The Fifth Michael Harding Memorial Address*, 1982, Reprinted 1985, London: Lesbian & Gay Christian Movement, ISSN: 0140 5993.

Boswell, John, *The Marriage of Likeness: Same-Sex Unions in Pre-Modern Europe*, 1995, London: Fontana Press, ISBN: 0 00 686326-4.

Buckley, Pat, *A Thorn in the Side*, 1994, Dublin: The O'Brien Press, ISBN: 0-86278-364-X.

Byrne, Lavinia, *Woman at the Altar: The Ordination of Women in the Roman Catholic Church*, 1994, London: Mowbray, ISBN: 0-264-67335-2.

Coote, Stephen (Ed.), *The Penguin Book of Homosexual Verse*, 1983 & 1986, London: Penguin Books.

Cozzens, Donald, *Sacred Silence: Denial and the Crisis in the Church*, 2002, Collegeville, Minnesota: The Liturgical Press, ISBN: 0-8146-2779-X.

Crowe, Thomas Rain, *Drunk on the Wine of the Beloved, 100 Poems of Hafiz*, 2001, Boston & London: Shambhala, ISBN: 1-57062-853-X.

Douglas, Nik, *Spiritual Sex: Secrets of Tantra from the Ice Age to the New Millennium*, 1997, New York, London: Pocket Books, ISBN: 0-671-53739-3.

Fox, Matthew, *Original Blessings: A Primer In Creation Spirituality*, 1983, Santa Fe, New Mexico, ISBN: 0-939680-07-6.

Fox, Matthew, *Confessions: The Making of a Post-Denominational Priest*, 1997, San Francisco: Harper, ISBN: 0-06-062865-0.

Fromm, Erich, *The Fear of Freedom*, 1984, London, Melbourne and Henley: Ark Paperbacks, ISBN: 0-7448-0014-5.

Gardner, Laurence, *Bloodline of the Holy Grail: The Hidden Lineage of Jesus Revealed*, 2000, Dorset, UK: Element, ISBN: 1-86204-726-X.

Hamilton, Phylis, with Paul Williams, *Secret Love: My Life with Father Michael Cleary*, 1995, Edinburgh and London: Mainstream Publishing, ISBN: 1-85158-8140.

Huebsch, Bill, with David Peterson, *A Radical Guide for Catholics: Rooted in the Essentials of our Faith*, 1996, Connecticut: Twenty Third Publications, ISBN: 0-89622-525-9.

Kennedy, Brian, *The Arrival of Fergal Flynn*, 2004, Dublin: Hodder Headline Ireland, ISBN: 0-340-83229-0.

Kung, Hans, *Why I am Still a Christian*, 1987, Edinburgh & New York: T&T Clarke, ISBN: 0-567-291340.

Ladinsky, Daniel, *The Subject Tonight Is Love: 60 Wild and Sweet Poems of Hafiz*, 1996, South Carolina: Pumpkin House Press, ISBN: 0-9657637-0-6.

Ladinsky, Daniel, *I Heard God Laughing: Renderings of Hafiz*, 1996, California: Sufism Reoriented, ISBN: 0-915828-18-9.

McNeill, John J., *The Church and the Homosexual*, 1993, Boston: Beacon Press, ISBN: 0 8070 7933 6.

McNeill, John J., *Taking a Chance on God: Liberating Theology for Gays, Lesbians and their Lovers, Families and Friends*, 1996, Boston: Beacon Press, ISBN: 0 8070 7945 6.

McNeill, John J., *Both Feet Firmly Planted: My Spiritual Journey*, 1998, Louisville, Kentucky: Westminster John Knox Press, ISBN: 0-664-25808-5.

Madden, Andrew, *Altar Boy: A Story of Life After Abuse*, 2003, Dublin: Penguin Ireland, ISBN: 1-844-88002-8.

Recommended Further Reading

Margolis, Jonathan, *"O": The Intimate History of the Orgasm*, 2004, London: Century, ISBN: 0-7126-2535-1.

Marinelli, L., *Shroud of Secrecy, The Story of Corruption within the Vatican*, 2003, Canada: Key Porter Books, ISBN: 1-55263-142-7.

Moore, Chris, *Betrayal of Trust: Father Brendan Smyth and the Catholic Church*, 1995, Dublin: Marino Books, ISBN: 1-86023-027-X.

Moore, Gareth, *A Question of Truth: Christianity and Homosexuality*, 2003, London: Continuum, ISBN: 0-8264-5949-8.

O'Connor, Alison, *A Message from Heaven: The Life and Crimes of Father Sean Fortune*, 2000, Kerry: Brandon, ISBN: 0-86322-270-6.

Ryan, Michael, *Secret Life: An Autobiography*, 1996, London: Bloomsbury, ISBN: 0-7475-3085-8.

Sipe, A.W. Richard, *Sex, Priests and Power, Anatomy of a Crisis*, 1995, London: Cassell, ISBN: 0-304-34638-1.

Sonkin, Daniel Jay, Ph.D, *Wounded Boys, Heroic Men: A Man's Guide to Recovering from Child Abuse*, 1998, Holbrook, Mass: Adams Media Corporation, ISBN: 1-580-62-010-8.

Stanford, Peter, *The She-Pope, A Quest for the Truth behind the Mystery of Pope Joan*, 1998, London: Arrow, ISBN: 0-7493-2067-2.

Stuart, Elizabeth Dr, *Daring to Speak Love's Name: A Gay and Lesbian Prayer Book*, 1992, London: Hamish Hamilton, ISBN: 0-241-13335-1.

Sullivan, Andrew, *Love Undetectable: Reflections on Friendship, Sex and Survival*, 1999, London: Vintage, ISBN: 0-09-927532-5.

Williams, Paul L., *The Vatican Exposed: Money, Murder and the Mafia*, 2003, New York: Prometheus Books, ISBN: 1-59102-065-4.